Twenty-five cents and GOD

by
Mary Mc Kenna

who also wrote
"The Family"

Copyright © 1982 by Thomas John Kondrak,
Minneapolis, Minnesota.
All Rights Reserved.

Printed in the United States of America.
No part of this publication may be reproduced,
stored in a retrieval system, or transmitted,
in any form or by any means, electronic, mechanical,
photocopying, recording, or otherwise, without the
prior written permission of the publisher.
The publisher's address is Brother De Paul Book Fund,
P.O. Box 2256, Minneapolis, Minnesota 55402 - 0256.

(For additional copies, please write to above address.)

Front cover design by Ted Maltese.

". . . Look at the birds: they do not plant seeds, gather a harvest . . . yet your Father in heaven takes care of them! Aren't you worth much more than birds? Can any of you live a bit longer by worrying about it?

. . . Look how the wild flowers grow. . . . But I tell you that not even King Solomon with all his wealth had clothes as beautiful as one of these flowers. . . . What little faith you have!

. . . Your Father in heaven knows that you need all of these things.

. . . So do not worry about tomorrow; it will have enough troubles of its own.

There is no need to add to the troubles each day brings."

       Words of JESUS of Nazareth
        (St. Matthew's Chapter 6)

Introduction From the Founder
About Whom This Book Is Written

This unusual narration, beginning with a twenty-five cent piece, is not intended to extol anyone's virtues, which fortunately for us are beneficient gifts of grace, but rather is intended to tell the ecumenical story of how it is genuinely possible in our scientific and technological 20th century to trust God in our daily lives — we call this trust in a fatherly, caring, providing God, trust in DIVINE PROVIDENCE.

It works today like it did in biblical times of old. This story should not be "preachy" but by living, real examples is meant to encourage others of all faiths or no faith, seeking any form of commitment to realize the Divine Power available in our lives *today*.

Although I am personally a loyal practicing and believing Catholic, this apostolate never was an official part of any institutionalized church or organization, but instead reveals how people of many denominations worked together as a big "family" to love and serve the poor, where ever they might be. And Flannery O'Connor forcefully reminds us that to be a believer one had to be willing to suffer from the church as well as for it. The church nowadays is considered as any assembled body of believers.

We have attempted in this biography to show God's love for *every* person everywhere without any kind of humanly made boundaries — and that out of this magnificent love has created each person as very special, fascinating and singular, worthy always of our respect and love, regardless of race, color, creed, position, sex, or what ever.

Every line in this book is meant to show the readers how much GOD loves each one of us . . . . and how lovingly HE takes care of us!!!!

DEDICATION

This unique, true biography is warmly dedicated from my heart to the beautiful and important women in my life:

TO:
> the gals of my auxiliaries and volunteers who shared with me and diligently labored to accomplish so much for our apostolate of love.

TO:
> my precious mother, Pauline Helen Nowak, to whom I am eternally indebted for her kind discipline and genuine sacrificial love.

TO:
> my dear sisters
>> Lucille Marie, who for the greatest part of her life, has cared for my semi-invalid mother besides her full time job.
>> Lillian Pauline and Yvonne Cecile who have also encouraged and supported me with their love.

TO:
> my dedicated and faithful, hard-working secretary, Alice Mary Codden, who has been my "right arm" for all of these years and whom I firmly believe God has placed in my life to assist me in the service of the needy.

And
TO:
> Christ's mother, Mary, whom God used as an instrument to provide us with a Saviour.

LOVINGLY and GRATEFULLY

dpk

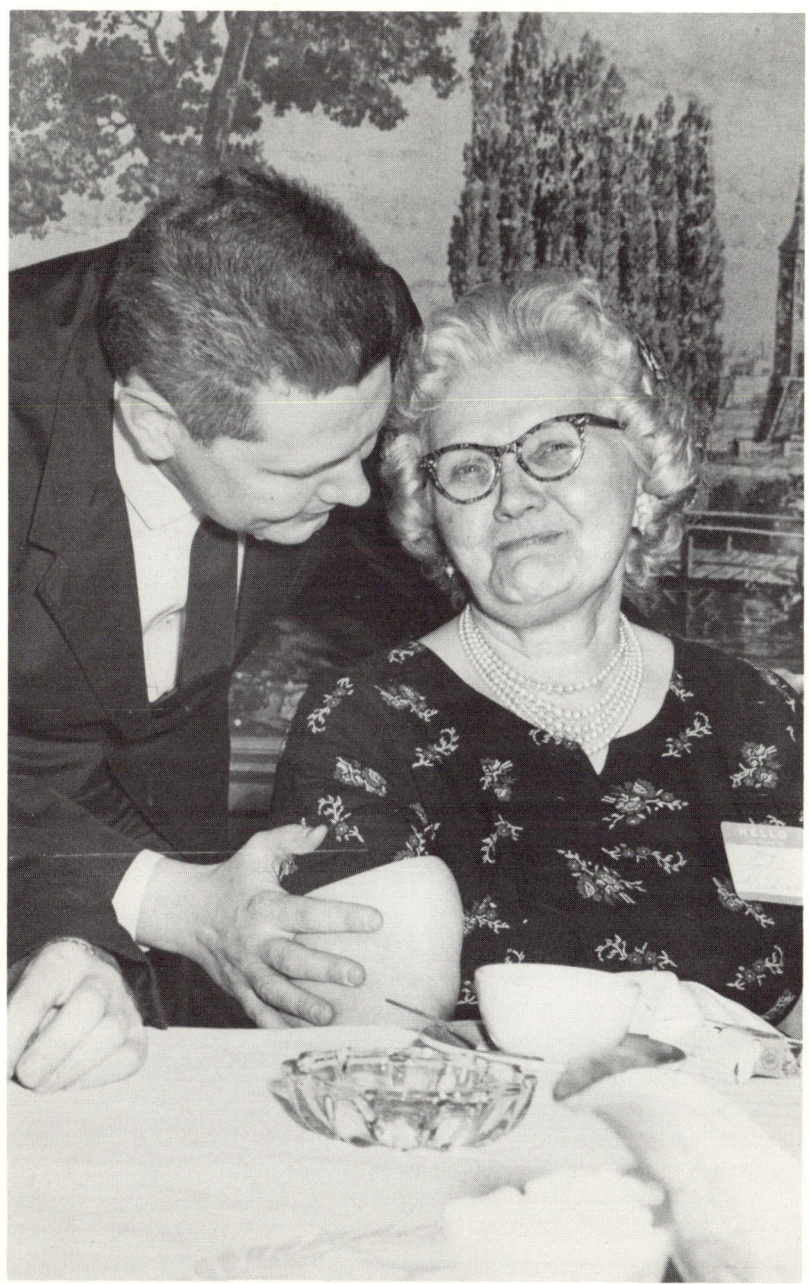

"Family Night" was a periodic, loving get-together of the residents, staff, and friends of the founder who is shown here with his dear mother at the Christmas party in 1965.

This was the place. I had parked my new Buick several blocks away, put on an old rain coat and babushka and walked to the "Food Centre" for a free meal. It was a single story building with a brick front, a white door with black hinges, a coach light beside the door, and a flag waving in the breeze. The Park Avenue address and the spelling of "Centre" seemed incongruous with the purpose of the place.

I saw several old men go into the building through the side door so I followed. I was nervous. "What if I'm stopped at the door? What if I run into someone I know?"

A thin, weathered man in a white shirt and a white baker's cap greeted me at the door. "Come right in, ma'am. You can go to the first table on the left." No questions.

Inside the Food Centre, I was amazed at the tasteful decor. Black wrought iron with scrolls and columns and circles divided the entry from the eating area. The walls of fruitwood paneling added warmth and furnished the background for a shrine of St. Anthony. There were about twenty formica-topped tables with eight or ten people seated at each. The cleanliness and orderliness of the workers and the recipients surprised me. Everyone, except me, seemed to know exactly what to do.

It seemed to be a social event where people met day after day and then disappeared in their separate directions. When one of the workers announced that volunteers were needed to help clean up, several responded. Were they trying to pay for their meal? Or, was it a way to stay warm a little longer?

I sat at a table for ten. Each place had a large plate with a bowl of soup — carrots, cabbage, noodles — and a small amount of meat in it. There was a plastic knife, fork and spoon and a napkin with a piece of cake at each setting.

At both ends of the table were large bowls of French fried potatoes, of green beans, a plate stacked high with bread, and a pitcher of ice water.

I watched to learn the procedure. When I finished my soup, I also went down the middle aisle to get hot potatoes and gravy. As I stood in line I wondered why each person was there. A young white couple caught my eye. He had a two-year old boy strapped to his back and she was pregnant. Had he lost his job? Was he a student? Many Indian men and women and young girls with small children seemed to congregate as families. Did they come from Reservations and weren't they able to make it in the big city? There were some black, and many young and old white men. I'd like to have listened to each one tell his story.

Across from me, a woman in her sixties and her son bowed their heads in a silent prayer. When they spoke, I knew they were from the south. I thought, but didn't ask, "Why are you way up here in Minnesota?"

"Have y'all evah bin to the church neah heah that gives free clothes away evry Tuesday and Thursday? Y'all should go ovuh there tunight and git some clothes foah yursef."

I had tried to "dress down," but I didn't know I had succeeded so well.

Sitting next to me was an Indian man who ate in silence. Finally, he looked up and saw a friend. "Hey, Gus!" he called. Gus was walking toward the door, but, about the third time the Indian called his name, he heard and came over to our table. He put his arm around his friend and told him, "You're the nicest man I know. I haven't seen ya for over three months. Whatcha been doin'?"

"Drinkin'," answered the man next to me.

"That's what I've been doin' too." Gus mumbled, "I'll see ya 'round." He left.

My discomfort went away as I realized no one paid any attention to me. I was just one of the many hungry people the House of Charity feeds every day.

But who is Brother de Paul? Why is he called "Brother?" Where does all the food come from? Who are all the men who cook it and serve it? How long has this project been going on?

For answers to these and many other questions, I have challenged Brother de Paul's memory, listened to his tapes, read letters and newspaper articles, and talked to some of his co-workers, his volunteers, his family, his benefactors, and some of the people he has served.

Chapter 1

The idea for feeding God's poor started 40 years ago when Tommy Kondrak was a young boy. Now, as Brother de Paul, he has a story to tell.

> The Lord is faithful in all his words
> and holy in all his works.
> The Lord lifts up all who are falling
> and raises up all who are bowed down.
> The eyes of all look hopefully to you,
> and you give them their food in due season.
> You open your hand and satisfy
> the desire of every living thing.
>
> Psalm 145:13-16

As 13 year old Tommy Kondrak wandered through the Skid Row of Minneapolis with his younger brother Ted and his friend, John, he wondered if the Lord was doing a very good job of "raising those who are bowed down." It was December 8, 1942 — the feast of the Immaculate Conception. To these boys it meant a day off from Holy Cross School — the day the Catholic kids had downtown Minneapolis all to themselves. They could wander up and down Nicollet Avenue peering into the beautifully decorated windows of Daytons, Donaldsons, Woolworths, and Powers. Each store had a different Christmas theme.

Because they had no spending money, the boys did more wishing than buying. It was their annual day to leave Northeast Minneapolis for the bustling, colorful downtown.

As they walked — they had no streetcar fare — across Nicollet Island on the Mississippi River, down lower Hennepin and Washington Avenues, they saw the men and women wander from building to building, eyes hopeless, looking for a stray coin, a half-smoked cigarette, a bottle not quite empty, or a handout from a passerby. These forlorn souls battled the cold hour after hour with newspapers under their coats.

These were the forgotten, the alcoholics, the lonely, who lived and died within a 29 block area of cheap hotels, flophouses, missions, bars, pawn shops, whorehouses, warehouses, and the City Post Office.

When Minneapolis was barely 30 years old, in 1884, the city government passed an ordinance which established the patrol limits for liquor establishments, and this led to concentration of them in what was called the Gateway area. It was here that the first bridge connected the east and the west, and the railroads brought people to Minneapolis. By 1910, 109 liquor stores, bars and saloons flourished in this lower loop area. This was during the heyday of the railroad and the city fathers, wanting to improve the view for passengers arriving in Minneapolis in 1915, created the Gateway Park. An attractive public shelter building of Greco-Roman architecture for use as a tourist information center and comfort station was built across Washington Avenue from the old Nicollet Hotel. The chiselled message over its columned portico read: "The Gateway — More than her gates, the city opens her heart to you."

Skid Row (a term that started in Seattle, Washington, where a row of streets was used to skid lumber down to the bay waters) has had its ups and downs with the times in Minneapolis. During prohibition, many of the saloons were closed or changed to soft drink bars, but many more of them were fronts for illegal beer and whiskey. The Depression brought young and old drifters to the area and, when prohibition was repealed in 1933, the Gateway was back in business. For 25¢ or 35¢ men could find a bunk for the night and then get a meal at one of the missions.

In 1942, Minnesota was geared for war, and many of the men from Skid Row went to work in the defense industries. Buses would line up near the Gateway building to gather the workers and take them to their jobs. This left the unemployable, the pensioners, the alcoholics, and a small stream of footloose drifters who were just passing through town following the seasons.

Tom, Ted, and John noticed these derelicts, these people cast off by society, but other than a smile, they had nothing to give. The sadness of these men and women struck a note in Tom's mind and heart.

After several hours of window shopping, the boys were cold and hungry, two good reasons for starting the long walk back home. As they trudged through Skid Row again, Tom yelled, "Look, guys, the sign says 'Free Lunch'! I'm starving." All three of them stopped to stare. A woman was putting sandwiches in the window. They rapped on the glass. "Could we have a sandwich, please?"

The lady came to the door, not smiling. "Don't you boys know this is a mission? If you want to come in for our service, then you can have a sandwich."

Tom and his buddies didn't know what a mission was, nor what the services were, but they turned down the offer. Tom peeked into the building and saw a statue of Christ. "Why do you have a statue of Jesus in there? He fed the hungry, didn't he?"

"Yes," the lady said impatiently, "and so do we, but first we read about Him, then we talk about Him, and then we sing to Him. It lasts about an hour and a half — then everyone is ready to eat. Maybe you boys can come back another day."

"Uh - no. Uh - no, thank you," Tom stammered, as they backed away from the mission door. As the trio walked home, Tom wondered aloud, "Why don't they just feed those hungry people? Why do they have to sit through a long service first?" He didn't realize then that a seed was being planted that eventually would grow into his life's work — helping the Lord "give them their food in due season."

Chapter 2

In 1943, when Tom graduated from the eighth grade at Holy Cross School, he was determined to go to De La Salle High School, a Catholic boys' school on Nicollet Island. The tuition would be a problem. Tom was the second of six children, at that time, and there was no money for such extras. Even at this early age, he trusted in God's providence. He would find a job and earn his tuition. At De La Salle, he would be right next to the Skid Row area, right next to many of the missions: the Union Gospel Mission, Faith Mission, Revival Mission, Harvest Field Mission, the St. James Hotel, the Salvation Army, plus many small short-lived missions.

As Tom walked through this area every day, he thought, "Why aren't there any places that feed and clothe and house these men without obliging them to worship?"

He saw hungry men bending over garbage cans in alleys behind restaurants. He heard the wail of sirens and saw city ambulances pick up drunk men from the gutters. He gave his hard-earned dimes to old men in dirty clothes who wanted to buy a bowl of soup. What he saw bothered him. "How can I help these men?" he asked himself.

This was wartime. Tom's father was working as a loader 365 days of the year at Pillsbury Mills, but Tom decided he could help his family too. As one of six children, he knew what it was like not to have enough food. He plowed, planted, weeded and harvested vegetables from his Victory Garden. All weekends and evenings during the summer, while other fifteen and sixteen-year old boys played nearby, Tom worked in his garden. He also raised pigeons, rabbits, and chickens for meat and eggs. He learned to tithe — ten percent of everything he produced he gave to the Little Sisters of the Poor. During the week, he worked in a box factory to earn his tuition for De

La Salle. From this grueling experience, Tom learned one thing after many smashed thumbs and lopsided boxes: he was not a carpenter.

Then, like the sun breaking through the clouds, the war was over. V-J Day, August 15, 1945, Minneapolis danced down Nicollet Avenue to celebrate peace. Tom, with three girl friends, joined the happy throng. Although too young to be in the war, they were old enough to comprehend the peace.

In 1946, Minnesota was in the throes of a polio epidemic. For several years Sister Elizabeth Kenny, the hardworking bush nurse from Australia, had been using her method of hot packing and passive exercise to prevent paralysis in polio victims. She had had an uphill battle proving to the medical world that her therapy was effective. Finally, the Sister Kenny Institute was established and, by 1946, was bulging with patients.

Tom Kondrak and his friends at school heard about Sister Kenny and they felt Minneapolis was lucky to have her.

"How can we show her how we feel?" one of the boys asked Tom.

"Well, I suppose if we were rich we could give her money to help her with her work. But we're not rich," Tom answered.

His friend thought awhile. "You know, Tom, we could make some money for her. How about having a benefit for Sister Kenny?"

And so the "Sister Kenny Twelve" was born. Tom and eleven boys from De La Salle and girls from various high schools rented a hall in Northeast Minneapolis. They talked the owner into no down payment. They advertised that there would be music for dancing and a free lunch. The plans sounded great, but one realist asked, "Where will we get the food?"

Tom had the answer. "We'll beg for it." And they did. A soda pop company, a potato chip factory and a baking company provided the "free" lunch.

They charged 50¢ a ticket and had to turn some of the people away. After the rent and music were paid for, they cleared $100. The Sister Kenny Twelve were proud to take this money to her office, expecting to put it into her hand. Unfortunately, she was not there. This was Tom's first experience with fund raising and he was pleased.

It had been 14 years since the last hardbound yearbook had been issued at De La Salle. Tom and a dozen classmates, with the help of Brothers Edward and Alphonsus, produced the 1946 Delta. They dedicated it to those who had died in the war — the De La Salle gold-star men — and their families.

The boys sold advertising to help pay the cost of paper and printing. They got publicity by presenting a copy to the Mayor of Minneapolis, Hubert H. Humphrey. This was the first of many meetings between Tom and this young politician who asked Tom to work for him. Although impressed with Humphrey's dynamic personality, Tom was not ready for politics. Tom had some of the same qualities as the mayor, tirelessness and love for people. His sister Lucille remembers that when she was 10 years old Tom was always "doing for others." At one time he converted an old shoe shop into a hall for teenage gatherings and dances. "He was always an organizer."

Chapter 3

In 1948, Tom's sister Vonnie was born. The whole family seemed to be thrilled to have a baby in the house again as the last child, Jerry, was eight.

Early in 1948, a girl who lived near the Kondraks gave Tom a book about the Lady of Fatima. In it, he read about the Blessed Mother's appearance to the three small children, Lucia, Jacinta, and Francisco in Fatima, Portugal.

On May 13, 1917, while they were tending their sheep, they saw a lady dressed in white, wearing a veil. She told them to come back on the 13th day of each month until October 13th when she would tell them who she was. Each month they saw her, and on October 13th, with 70,000 people watching, the sun spun around and power dived to the earth. She foretold that two of the little shepherds would die in childhood — and they did. She predicted the Bolshevik Revolution and the horrors of World War II. She told the children she was the Lady of the Rosary and she asked them to recite the rosary every day.

The rosary, a widely used form of prayer for Catholics, was first used in the early centuries of Christianity by many people who could not read the psalms. It consisted of stones or seeds strung on a cord. One "Our Father" and one "Hail Mary" were substituted for each of the 150 psalms. The "Our Father" is the prayer that Jesus taught His disciples in Matthew 6: 9-13: "Our Father, who art in Heaven, etc. The "Hail Mary" consists of two parts: "Hail Mary, full of grace, the Lord is with thee" were the words the Angel Gabriel spoke to Mary when he asked her to become the mother of Jesus. The words of St. Elizabeth when visited by Mary follow: "Blessed art thou among women, and blessed is the fruit of thy womb." — Luke 1:41-42. The second part of the "Hail Mary" was composed by the church:

"Holy Mary, Mother of God, pray for us sinners now and at the hour of our death."

In the 13th century, St. Dominic made the use of the rosary more widespread. The complete rosary was divided into three parts with five Our Fathers and 50 Hail Marys in each. The people were encouraged to meditate, while praying the rosary, on the mysteries of the life, the passion and the glorification of the Lord.

The Lady said that if peace were to be gained in the world, there would have to be prayer and penance.

Tom was so impressed by the story of Fatima that he wanted to tell others about it. He approached the associate pastor at Holy Cross Church, Father Edward Szymanski. "I love the Lady of Fatima. How can I spread her message about praying the rosary every day? Who can I tell?"

Father Szymanski explained to Tom that the Blessed Mother's appearance at Fatima was a private revelation, just as at Lourdes and Guadalupe. Although, after thorough investigation, the church approved the story of Fatima, it never obliged its followers to believe it.

"But, Tom, I think your best bet would be to talk to other high school kids. When they hear someone their own age asking them to pray and do penance, they may pay attention."

He did this. At De La Salle, at St. Anthony's, St. Margaret's, and Holy Angels High Schools in Minneapolis and Cathedral High in St. Cloud, this gangly kid spoke. Sometimes girls he had dated giggled as Tom told about the Lady of Fatima and her request for each of them to pray the rosary and do penance for peace.

Then he went to parish groups to tell his story. He formed a Fatima Group which met every week to spread devotion to the Lady of the Rosary. He started the International Peace Program on Radio WMIN where he gave a short message on Fatima, and each decade of the rosary was recited in a different language. The Fatima group was so moved by Tom's enthusiasm that they started a collection to send him to Portugal.

This endeavor was led by Helen Drellack, one of his most loyal and hard working members of the Fatima Group. Many of their meetings and activities were held in her home in northeast Minneapolis. She wrote letters asking for contributions for Tom's trip to Portugal, saying that "Tom should see what he is talking about." She had a party for him at the Northeast Neighborhood House. This caused a little flak because this house was then considered a "Protestant Center," and ecumenism had not yet been heard of. The priest from Holy Cross Church complained to Tom's father, "and your son let Helen Drellack give a benefit for him in the Northeast Neighborhood House. Shame!" John Kondrak chided his son, but this was the first of many of Tom's projects that his father disapproved of.

In July of 1949, Tom flew to Fatima. This was his first plane trip, and after the initial shock of taking off from the ground, he loved it. He saw his first mountain, and he was awestruck by their beauty, their majesty and their strength. Then he was at Fatima — right where he believed the Blessed Mother of Jesus appeared to the three shepherd children. He was so inspired with the shrine, with the atmosphere, and with other pilgrims who had come to pray, that he was more determined than ever to spread Mary's message for peace in the world. While he was at Fatima, he photographed a woman who had been cured of paralysis on the left side of her body. He didn't give her too much thought until a week after he got home. He had gone on to Rome, but had flown back to Minneapolis a few days early because he had run out of money.

Tom's younger brother Ted was home when his mother, who had been baking in the kitchen, fell to the floor in a seizure. In a few minutes, she lay relaxed, and insisted he should not call the doctor. Several days later, as she was hanging clothes outside, this happened again. This time Ted did call the doctor who said, "It's probably a sun stroke, but bring her into the hospital." They took her to St. Barnabas Hospital where the seizures continued and she became paralyzed on the left side of her body. Then Tom remembered the picture he had taken at Fatima. What did it mean?

Pauline Kondrak was moved to the University Hospital where the doctors did all kinds of tests. Was it a stroke or encephalitis or what? There was no end to the seizures and whoever stayed with her had to hold a taped tongue depressor in her mouth most of the time. The doctors considered her age, 44, her young children, Vonnie was only a year old, and they decided to try surgery. Opening the top of her head relieved the pressure and stopped the seizures, but her prognosis was grim. She lay motionless and the doctors said she probably wouldn't be able to see, to talk, or to walk. They gave her two years to live.

Tom took the night shift to stay with his mother at the hospital, and during the day he took care of his brothers and sisters at home. He took care of Vonnie as a parent would. One day he took her to the hospital to see their mother, and for the first time since her surgery, Pauline smiled.

After four months of lying still, she started to respond to therapy. She gradually began to see, to talk, and after many months of rehabilitation from wheelchair, to crutches, to walker and finally to a cane, she was able to walk.

In 1952, John and Pauline celebrated their 25th wedding anniversary in their living room with all their children. They renewed their vows and received Holy Communion from Father Szymanski. The family gave them their first refrigerator.

For over thirty years, Tom's sister Lucille has heroically cared for her mother who is still partially paralyzed. She has dressed her, fixed her hair, and made her ready for the day before herself going to work.

Chapter 4

While Tom was going to the University of Minnesota, he worked long hours during the summer to save money for his tuition, book fees and car fare. He was a plumber's assistant, he worked in a sausage factory, he cleaned stores at night and he was a janitor at Northern States Power Company.

No matter how he scrimped he never had enough money for clothes. His mother and father were buying their first home, so he couldn't ask them for help. But Tom didn't give up easily. He contacted Kay Bonner who produced a show in Dayton's small auditorium for WTCN Radio every Saturday morning, "Soda Set," for teenagers. He talked her into giving him a few minutes of air time to tell the results of Friday night High School games. In payment, each week he could pick out an item of clothing. He earned a great collection of "sharp" sweaters, shirts, trousers, and jackets. He was a poor but well-dressed student.

While he was on "Soda Set" Tom met some guests who were celebrities — the Harmonicats and Liberace were among them.

As Tom met with the Fatima group to talk about Mary, he realized he had the nucleus that could help him serve the poor. He asked them for food and clothing whenever he found someone in need. He visited some of the parishioners at St. Leonard's Church and brought them whatever he could beg. One of the first projects for the Fatima group was to bring 40 kids to a picnic. The members were surprised when they arrived at Como Park and found the 40 children were black. Tom had met them while visiting at St. Leonard's.

In the spring of 1952 Tom began to work full time at St. Leonard's. He taught the children catechism, he was the janitor, he rang the bell for the

Angelus calling people to pray in the morning, at noon, and in the evening, he visited the parishioners, he answered the phone and he took charge whenever the pastor, Father Leonard Hirman, went out of town. He did this for $25 a month and a lot of personal satisfaction. He learned what it was to be hungry.

When Helen Drellack, the dedicated woman from Tom's Fatima group was offered a job as Father Hirman's housekeeper, she offered Tom her house as a base for his work. He remembered how Helen, who worked all day as a dishwasher at Sleizer's Club, had come in to sit all night with his mother after surgery. Because of a polio epidemic, it had been almost impossible to get a nurse. Helen had a simple faith, a spontaneous generosity.

Tom was overwhelmed with her offer of her home, but not for long. He had 25¢ in his pocket, a head full of dreams, and a lot of faith in God's providence.

FIRST HOUSE OF CHARITY located in Northeast Minneapolis.

He moved into Helen's house at 1506 2nd Street Northeast on July 4, 1952. He had a bed, a couch, a hot plate and a refrigerator. There was one floor heater for the whole house. The Fatima group had a painting party to redecorate the house and a shower to collect bedding. Mary Marino, a friend in the Fatima group, had the first benefit for Tom's work. She had mentioned to him that she would like to have a pizza party for him sometime. Flyers were out the next week telling about the benefit. He had scheduled it the same day as her parish picnic, but she couldn't back out. She made pizza and sold it in her home all Sunday afternoon. With the money, she put drapes in every room of his house.

Tom was comfortable in his new home but he was lonely. He had left his family home where there was always a lot of activity and he missed it. Both his father and mother had expressed their disappointment that their son, college educated, was not going "to make something of himself." They couldn't understand why he wanted to live with and beg for the poor.

Tom felt there was not enough to do in Northeast Minneapolis. He was too far from the people he wanted to help. He kept his job at St. Leonard's and had Fatima meetings, but he kept asking "What am I doing here all alone in this seven-room house?"

One hot Saturday in August, Tom walked the twelve blocks to his folks' home to hear the presidential convention. Since his family didn't approve of what their 23-year old was doing, not many words were spoken. They feared for his safety — working with "those people." Tom sat quietly until his 4 year old sister, Vonnie, whom he had taken care of as a baby, threw her arms around his neck and asked, "When are you coming home from your vacation, Tommy?"

"I'm not coming back, Vonnie," Tom answered sadly. As he walked back to 1506 his eyes were so full of tears, he wondered why he was going back to this house of nothing. He loved his little sister so much. "God, what are you doing to me?" He was tempted to give up his dream that night. Tom didn't go back to see his family for a long time — it was too painful.

John Kondrak, Tom's father, was born in Poland. When he was 22 years old, he came to Canada with his aunt and her children. He finally came to Minneapolis and went to work at Pillsbury Mills as a loader, a job he kept for 38 years. He worked hard, learned to speak English, and, when he was 36 years old, married Pauline. His family was his pride. During the depression, he worked only three days a week, but by making dumplings every other day, Pauline managed to feed their family. Lillian, Tommy, Ted, Don, Lucille, Jerry and at last, Vonnie, joined the parents in their small home in Northeast Minneapolis.

Being older than most fathers, John Kondrak took his obligations to his children very seriously. They would go to school, learn a trade or profession and make their own living.

Their son, Tom, didn't follow this pattern; and it bothered his father and mother. "Why do you want to waste your education living with poor people?" they asked him. Tom really had no answer they could understand. It was easier to avoid seeing them than to try to explain his mission to do God's work with the poor.

Chapter 5

After two months of living alone in his new home, Tom met Walter Groll. Walter was from Georgia, the son of a Baptist minister. While he had been in the Navy he had learned a little about Catholicism and he had wanted to learn more. He had sent for a correspondence course, and he had read "Father Smith Instructs Jackson." He had corresponded with the author of this book, Archbishop John Noll, and then had made his decision to become a Catholic.

Now Walter was working in a foundry in Minneapolis and he heard about Tom Kondrak from friends. Early in September he met Tom at St. Leonard's Church. They talked about their goals in life, they talked about the poor, and they talked about the providence of God. They discovered they thought alike about these things.

"Why don't you move to 1506 2nd Street Northeast and maybe we can work together for God's poor? He must have some plan for us." Tom met Archbishop John Gregory Murray and talked to him about starting a mission to feed the hungry. He explained how he had seen these poor people for years and had planned to help them. Tom wanted to call it the House of Love. The Archbishop, with a knowing look, advised his 23 year old visitor, "You might get the wrong people knocking at your door." He didn't like the suggested name and he gave Tom little encouragement. House of Charity became the name.

Walter moved in. As they prayed together, Tom had the feeling of "community." He thought of St. Francis of Assisi who had given up a life of wealth to beg for the poor. This 13th century saint had loved people. He had loved the leper, whom he had hugged and given money to; the man suffering from the cold to whose shoulders he had transferred his own cloak;

the robbers to whom he had given his goods. The eleven companions who had joined Francis in begging food for the poor had become the nucleus of the great religious order — the Franciscans.

Tom and Walter decided they would follow the rule of the Third Order of St. Francis. They took private temporary vows of poverty, chastity and obedience, and followed the prayer life of the Third Order. This included the 5 decades of the rosary, the Third Order office, which is a group of different psalms for worship and praise each day, 15 minutes of silent meditation and 30 minutes of spiritual reading.

That was the beginning of Tom's dream. St. Vincent de Paul, the French saint who was the patron of charitable societies, had alwalys inspired him because he was known for his organizing ablility in serving the poor. In this spirit Tom became Brother de Paul. Walter became Brother Martin, after the black saint from Peru, St. Martin de Porres. They both kept their jobs for a few months, Brother de Paul at St. Leonard's and Brother Martin at the foundry, but they took time for collecting clothes for poor families, meeting with the Fatima group and prayer.

Shortly after Brother Martin moved in, he came home from the foundry one evening hot and sweaty from working in the heat all day. He took a cold bath because there was no hot water and became very sick. Brother de Paul rushed him to St. Mary's Hospital where he almost died of pneumonia.

"But that was providential," Brother de Paul said many years later. "While I was on my way to see Brother Martin, I saw a sign on Nicollet Island, 'Building for Sale — $12,500.' We felt we had to be located closer to the center of the city to do our work." $12,500! Brother de Paul had no money, and Brother Martin had a $251 hospital bill; but in his naivete Tom approached Mr. Rohne, the owner. "Would you be willing to take less?"

"$11,500 cash is rock bottom."

"I don't want to buy or rent," Brother tried to explain, "something in between."

When Brother de Paul told Mr. Rohne that he had no money and the House of Charity couldn't get a loan, but he would like to have the keys to the building, the man stared in disbelief. After a few moments the owner said, "I must be crazy. Here, take the keys." They paid nothing for the first few months.

The building in its time had been an ice cream factory, a Volunteers of America store, a gambling house and a house of prostitution. Now, old and abandoned, its foundations were cracking. But it was in the right place, Brother de Paul thought, for him and Brother Martin to expand their House of Charity. Helen Drellack's son had come home from the service and wanted to live in his mother's house, so a move was imperative.

This was Brother's first trust in God for big things. As he looked over the filthy, cold, barren building, he wondered what the Lord had in store for him.

Brother Martin was still in the hospital so Brother de Paul spent his first night at 26 East Hennepin alone. It was October and, without any heat, it was cold. The dim lights cast scary shadows, the mice scrambled around seeming to resent this intruder, a bat swooped down over his cot, and it was lonely. "My God, what am I doing here?"

The birth of Brother de Paul's House of Charity was a painful and lonely experience. He felt, and a fire seared his insides. He pitied, and the anguish of it brought tears to his eyes. He acted, and the first step on a long and difficult road began.

Chapter 6

Nicollet Island had been a fashionable section of Minneapolis in the last quarter of the nineteenth century, but by 1900 many of the old families, the Eastmans, Kings, Bassetts, and de Laitrres among others, had sold out and left the Island. It declined as a residential neighborhood. The absentee landlords wouldn't invest money for the upkeep of the once stately houses that were divided into apartments and rooming houses. The main street of the Island, East Hennepin Avenue, became the haunt of the transient and the alcoholic. These were some of God's people the Brothers wanted to serve. In 1952, the year that Brother de Paul started the House of Charity, the Minneapolis Parks Superintendent inspected the Gateway Building which had been so ceremoniously dedicated in 1915 with its chiseled message of welcome over its portico. He found 200 whiskey and wine bottles nearby. Its tourist information center was gone; the comfort station was called the "pisshouse," and the view from the train station of all the poor men sitting around it gave the Park Board the nudge to give the Gateway Park a new look. This was the beginning of the ten-year demolition and rebuilding of Skid Row — right next to Nicollet Island.

Before Brother Martin could come "home" from the hospital, Brother de Paul had to get a stove for heat. A woman donated one. Then he had to beg for coal. He got that. But the one stove couldn't take care of the five rooms of the upper floor. The oven was left open to give the maximum heat, and the two men slept in winter coats but were still cold. Many times the water pipes froze, and every morning the water in the toilet bowl was ice. Bath water was heated in a small hot water heater.

Brother Martin recovered in spite of these discomforts, and he was ready to join Brother de Paul in his ministry. They began by asking for leftovers from restaurants, day-old bread from bakeries, and small donations from friends. They took some of this food to families in St. Leonard's Church, where Brother de Paul had worked since spring. Through these black families he had learned of the miserable life of some of the railroad porters and dining car waiters who lived above the stores on Washington Avenue — as many as ten or twelve in two small rooms. When the Brothers arrived with food and clothes for these men, they practically tore it out of their hands. Brother de Paul had never seen such poverty among workers.

Several weeks into October Brother de Paul announced, "Brother Martin, we're going to feed and house anyone who comes to us."

Brother Martin was stunned. "Brother de Paul, you must be crazy! Where will we get the food? What will they sleep on? We don't have any beds."

"Trust, Brother, trust in God."

FIRST PHOTO AT HOUSE OF CHARITY — this shows Brother de Paul, seated, registering overnight guests on Nicollet Island in 1952.

They began to feed five or six men and half of them came back to spend the night. They didn't seem to mind sleeping on the floor with coats and blankets to keep from freezing. Their alternative was either a box car or a flop house. Eventually, there were as many as 17 men on the floor. In the morning they were given coffee, a roll or cereal and sent on their way. Many of them washed and shaved in the morning, but on Saturday night the two Brothers reserved the hot water for themselves and their baths. They felt grimy after a week, day and night, in the same clothes. Brother de Paul almost jumped out of the tub the night he discovered his body covered with lice. He sent Brother Martin to the drug store to get "blue ointment" and he threw his clothes out into the alley to be burned.

By Thanksgiving Day, barely six weeks after the House of Charity began operating on Nicollet Island, word had spread that free food was available. Brother Martin used his experience as a cook in the service to put together soup with rice, bread and pudding for dessert. Feeding five at a time around their small table, cleaning up, and resetting for another five, the two men fed 75 people. It took them three hours. They were tired, but they were thankful.

The first time Brother Martin went out to beg for food, one of his stops was at Lakeland Produce. To test his sincerity, the produce man said, "Before we give you anything, you have to work for it." He had to unload vegetables from a box car. Several hours later he trudged home, tired, with blistered hands, but loaded down with fresh vegetables. Lakeland continued to donate fresh foods every week until they went out of business.

Early in December, the Founder began planning the Christmas dinner. He was going to serve the traditional meal — turkey, dressing, potatoes, gravy, rolls, pie and coffee. He would also beg for clothing and toys all over town to share with the poor families at St. Leonard's, or anyone else who needed them.

When Brother Martin asked Brother de Paul where they would get a complete turkey dinner for the people who would come on Christmas, the founder gave his stock answer, "Trust, Brother, trust in God." And it worked! He contacted his friend, Doris Sneider, who had invited him and Brother Martin to her restaurant for a good meal several times in the last few months. "Don't worry, Brother," she said "I'll get what you need, and I'll even bake the turkeys at my restaurant."

Mariely Adler had been a bell ringer for the Salvation Army's Christmas effort. For about a month before Christmas she'd stood by the kettle in the Main Post Office collecting money to buy food and gifts for "the poor people."

"Tvice a day, dese two young men vould valk by me," this petite 80 year old lady recounted in her Swiss-German accent, "but do you tink dey vould look at me? Dey looked straight ahead, and I tought to myself, 'My goodness, I don't vant anyting you got. You could at least say hello.''

"Dey kept valking by me day after day vidout turning der heads. Den vun day dey ver by da door in front of me ven a priest came in. He made da sign of da cross above der heads, and after dat dey smiled at me and said hello. I don't tink dat priest knew dey ver so obstinate, and I don't tink da boys knew da priest blessed dem, but it vorked!

"I told dem dey didn't have to give me anyting for my kettle, just a smile for me. I tink dey needed money more den I did. Dat vas ven dey ver starting da House of Charity and dey probably tought I should be ringing da bell for dem.

"Da first time I really met Brother de Paul vas at a Salvation Army mens' social 10 years later. My husband, Fritz, vorked vit men who ver homeless and drinking too. I vas so happy to see him and I asked him if he remembered me. 'Do you know how ve met?' I asked.

"He remembered and he laughed, Den he asked, 'Vill you come to da dinner we are having for our benefactors and tell dem how ve met?' I did, and ve have been friends ever since.

"My husband did da same kind of vork as Brother de Paul, and he alvays enjoyed talking vit him. You haf to have your heart in dat kind of vork or you vould be a traitor. My husband just died and I miss him very much. Ve ver married for over 55 years."

One day before Christmas a card and a check arrived in the mail. The Women's Altar Society from St. Joseph's Church in Hopkins, Minnesota sent $100! "Wow!" Brother yelled, "Now we can pay some of our bills!" Another envelope arrived from St. Mary's Hospital. "Paid in full, Merry Christmas, Sisters of St. Mary's."

There was very little heat, very little hot water — just a lot of love that went into that first Christmas on Nicollet Island. The Brothers had four burners and a small oven to keep the food hot for 75 men.

Early Christmas morning, a poorly clad mother knocked on the door at the House of Charity begging for food for her family. Every wrinkle showed the struggle she had in giving them mere necessities. Brother de Paul fixed her a tray of food to take home and gave her some toys for her children. Just the way she gripped these treasures showed Brother her gratitude.

The table in the small dining room now fed six at a time. They led each group in grace, served them a delicious dinner, washed the plates and silverware, reset the table and served another six people. They did this a dozen times and it took most of the afternoon.

Midway through the Christmas dinner, a suburban police car pulled up to the House of Charity and the officers rushed in. "Could you please give us some food for a couple who don't have a thing to eat?"

"Of course."

Toward evening, the Brothers began to welcome the men who would stay for the night, men who had no home, no shelter. It reminded Brother de Paul of Bethlehem in its simplicity. He and Brother Martin felt close to God that Christmas night because they thought He had performed a miracle, giving them what they needed to provide Christmas for the poor.

One man, just under 21, wanted to talk at length about his boxing career. The Brothers listened. A man in his 70's, shivering from the cold, wanted to join the other 17 men who were scattered throughout the house on the floors. Brother de Paul told him, "We have no beds, and it's cold in here."

"I don't mind," he said. "I know you care about me."

Fifteen years later Brother de Paul was asked by the Editor of the Minneapolis Tribune to share his thoughts about his most memorable Christmas, that first Christmas on Nicollet Island in 1952:

"After everyone was as comfortable as possible under these conditions, I greeted them for the last time with a rather tired 'Merry Christmas' and prepared to turn off the lights of the small Christmas tree given us by a

neighbor. A handsome, ruggedly built man in his mid-50's boyishly begged me to leave the lights on. "Please, Brother, leave the tree lighted; it's our only Christmas."

"An old gentleman with a heavy Scandinavian accent beckoned me to him, pressing into my hands his magnanimous gift, a homemade needle threader composed of a popsicle stick and wire.

"Almost exhausted from sharing the life and misery of our guests, I knelt on the cold floor . . . praying, as I looked over the crouched, sleeping figures of 18 men. They were symbols of those who were to become the heart of my existence for 15 years to come — transients, former prisoners, alcoholics, the aged and the sick.

"I glanced up at the tree which now looked better and brighter than the traditional giant tree in Rockefeller Plaza.

"As I lay on my cot with my overcoat and three blankets wrapped around me in preparation for the long cold night, I thanked the newborn Savior for giving me the vocation of serving others. I knew by my faith that I had seen Him many times that day in the person of those in need, as if I had pilgrimaged to Bethlehem itself.

"As I turned over on my cot, one of the guests informed me that the water pipes were frozen in the rest room. I had shared, too, the poverty of the stable. I was happy on Nicollet Island. There were carols in my heart that late Christmas night in 1952."

Chapter 7

The men were never questioned. It didn't matter if they were black or red or white, whether they were believers or unbelievers. The House of Charity was for those who were hungry, lonely, broke or down on their luck.

Since Brother de Paul's experience with missions 10 years before, he was determined to offer warmth, Christian fellowship and free food without preaching. He had heard men talk about having to listen to a preacher for an hour, "ear banging" — then "singing for their supper" — then "coming to the altar" so they would get a bed for the night. He wanted none of this in the House of Charity. A short prayer of thanks to God for the food and those who donated it, cooked it and served it.

"The men will feel Christ's presence through our work," Brother de Paul thought, "because it is induced, inspired and encouraged by our love for Him."

The Brothers' day was long. They got up at 5:45, early enough to have coffee, a roll or doughnut and sometimes cereal ready for the men who had spent the night with them. Then they opened the doors to whoever was hungry. After feeding all the men and sending them on their way, Brother Martin and Brother de Paul walked over to Our Lady of Lourdes Church for mass. Back to their chilly building for a quick breakfast, and after cleaning the five rooms, they went out to beg for food, clothing, coal, furniture and anything they needed. Childlike they trusted God to provide the people who would support and provide their material needs to carry on His work.

For the first few months their main support had come from a handful of friends in the Fatima group. At their meetings they had passed the hat to pay the telephone bill of $2.63. Later one of these providers was the Master Bakery on 29th and Park Avenue, about three miles from the House of Charity. The Brothers had no car so they took turns going out on the streetcar. They picked up two large cartons of bread, 24 loaves in each, and as they transferred from one streetcar to another, they got some dirty looks for taking up so much room. Some conductors asked for an extra fare. The Brothers were embarrassed because they didn't have it. They were also getting food from Taystee Bakery, Acme Box Lunch, McGlynn Bakeries, Cafe di Napoli and parish dinner left-overs.

By mid-afternoon Brother de Paul and Brother Martin had to begin fixing the evening meal which was served at 5:30, that is, the first five or six were fed then. Usually a line of men waited on the stairway leading up to the second floor dining room. Forty to 60 men would come every night so the Brothers reset the table eight to 10 times. It took all evening to feed these hungry men, who would then lie down on the floor and cover themselves with their coats for the night. The House of Charity's five rooms were their whole world and the Brothers' too. Brother de Paul felt total happiness living with the poor without even a radio or television. Administration consisted of a record of meals served and names of the men who stayed.

Before he and Brother Martin said their night prayers, they set up the coffee pot to be started in the morning and they set the table for breakfast. By 10:25 p.m. they were exhausted as they grabbed a coat or two to wrap around themselves as they slept on the hard floor.

Brother de Paul and Brother Martin were among the few young people at mass every morning at Our Lady of Lourdes Church. They introduced themselves to the pastor, Father Anthony Chouinard, and told him about their work on Nicollet Island. They also invited him to visit the House of Charity.

When he finally came, he inspected their meager quarters, and as he opened the lean pantry, he raised his hand in blessing and prayed, "Dear God, may the House of Charity never be without food." This prayer has always been answered, as they've served millions of meals. Sometimes the larder has become low and they didn't know where the food would come from, but they knew it would come. The House of Charity has never accepted money from the government, any organized church, or any philanthropic institution or foundation. With God's providence they were located on a main street, East Hennepin Avenue, with seven bus lines. They were very visible to people passing by. Also in God's providence, "the better we fed and the less we stored, the more God provided."

Chapter 8

In January of 1953, Brother de Paul took the bus to Greeley, Kansas to speak about the Fatima message. He told the group about his work with the new House of Charity. "We have a big building to use for our feeding of the poor," he lamented, "but it's cold. We have a four burner cook stove to heat five rooms."

His audience responded. They took up a collection for a gas furnace, and it was installed immediately.

Every morning that winter, when Brother de Paul and Brother Martin came home from mass, they would prostrate themselves on their small chapel floor to thank God for heat. They even had a thermostat.

One evening in early January, Monsignor Joseph Sieginski, the pastor of Holy Cross Church, called the House of Charity. "May I speak to Brother de Paul, please?"

"This is Brother de Paul."

"Brother, this is Monsignor Sieginski from Holy Cross Church. Do you remember the life size statue of Christ which was in our school hallway?"

Did he remember! Every day for eight years he had marched past this statue of Christ. He could almost see the double line of kids marching in rank as Sister Emanuel played a record. He had never realized what an important place it would take in his life.

"Yes, Monsignor, I remember it well."

"I'm wondering if you would like to have the statue?"

"I'd love to have it," the founder said excitedly.

"It's quite old, you know. It was imported from France for the old Holy Cross Church. When that was torn down, the statue was moved to the school. Because you grew up in this parish, I thought you might appreciate it."

"Oh, I would, Monsignor. Thank you for thinking of me and for what this personal gift of encouragement means to me." The statue of Christ became the symbol of the House of Charity. A picture of it has been used on Christmas cards and letters of appeal. It was placed in a lighted window for all to see — Christ with his hand pointing to his heart. Men all over the country have told their fellow vagrants, "Go to the place in Minneapolis that has Christ in the window."

One day, a young man on his way to work at the House of Charity was picked up by the police on Hennepin Avenue after he got off the bus. He was booked as a vagrant because he had no money and sent to the workhouse. This angered Brother de Paul. He thought this was done just to get needed workers to do the farm work.

Several days later, Brother Martin gave a birthday party for Brother de Paul. He invited his friends and everyone who had helped at the House of Charity. He also invited the Mayor of Minneapolis, Eric Hoyer.

After thanking the Mayor and all his friends for coming to his birthday party, Brother de Paul brought up the injustice of picking up vagrants. He always had a sense of justice and spoke out for it when necessary. This brought him and the House of Charity public attention.

A few weeks later, Cedric Adams, a local newscaster and newspaper columnist, talked about the House of Charity's ramshackle building and its need for donations. Everyone in the area listened to Cedric. Airline pilots flying over Minnesota knew when his newscast was over — all the lights in the farmhouses went off. The photographer on his telecast panned the statue of the Lady of Fatima, and Cedric told about Brother de Paul's trip to the shrine. They were becoming known gradually.

While the volunteers were partitioning the front window and building an appropriate platform for the statue of Christ they continued their work on the first floor by painting the lobby and remodeling a room for a dormitory. All the knotty pine paneling was donated by Scherer Brothers Lumber Company. Old wall paper was removed, filthy walls were washed and painted in the room adjoining the lobby, so that by June it was suitable to be used as a 13-bed dormitory. "But we have no beds!" Brother Martin wailed even before the room was finished. Brother de Paul searched every possible source for free beds, and finally the word got to the right place. The Sisters at St. Elizabeth's convent were replacing their beds and had about 15 to give away.

"God's providence again, Brother Martin," Brother de Paul panted as he helped set up the old brass beds. Each night of the week the beds were full. The men joked about sleeping in the nuns' beds.

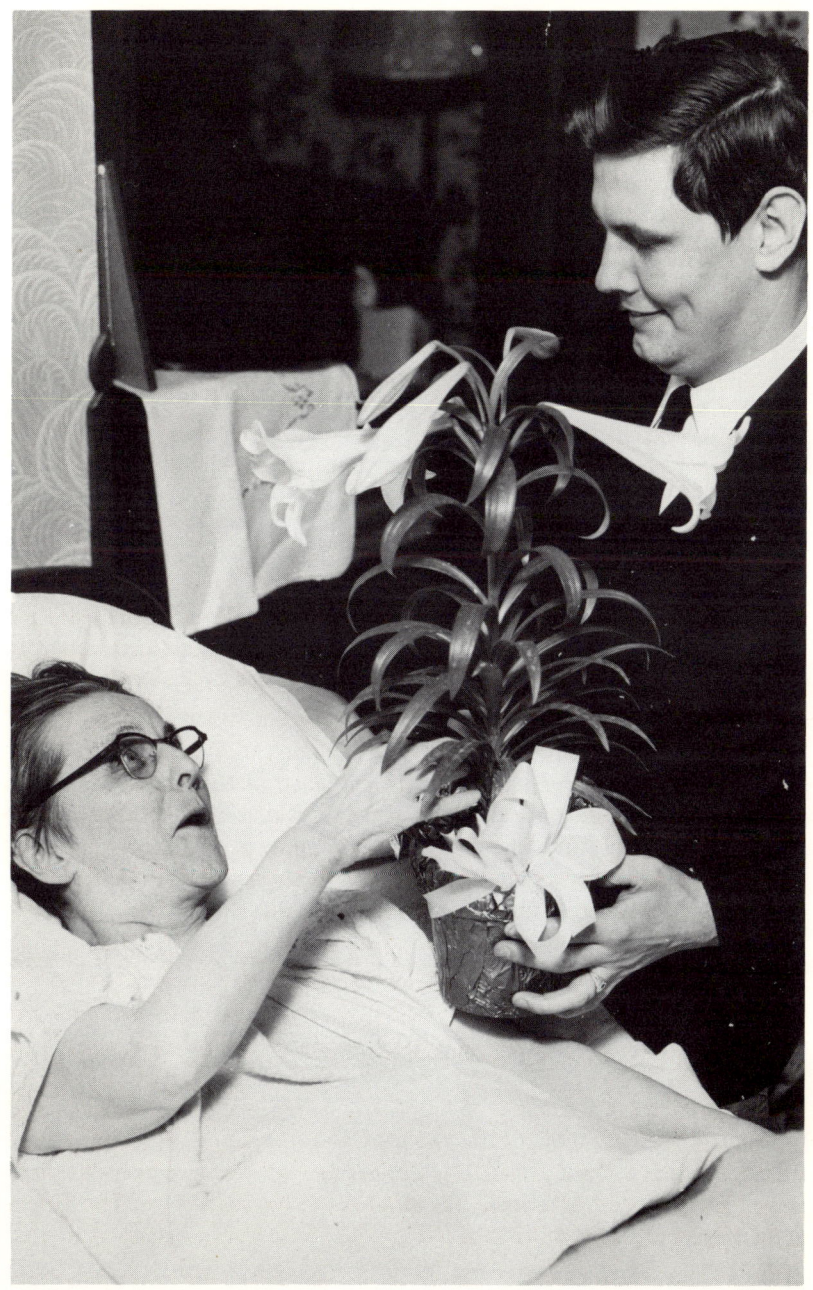

O! WHAT A BEAUTIFUL LILY exclaims Regina Bolduc, a shut-in bedridden for over 30 years. This photo shows the founder on one of his many visits to the sick and handicapped persons, his favorite project in "off hours."

By 1953 there were about 3000 residents plus many transients in the Skid Row area. The alternative to sleeping at the House of Charity or the Salvation Army was grim — flophouses with 5x7 feet chicken wire cages, box cars or under a bridge. The men came in by 9:30 p.m., signed their name and city, and were given the location of their bed. Many slept in all their clothes. The sheets had to be washed every day — in a donated wringer washer. As the Brothers stripped the beds they checked for bed bugs and, if they found any, they treated the bedding and the mattresses. They hung the sheets outside and sometimes they were still drying at eight o'clock at night. Many years later, when someone gave the House of Charity a clothes dryer, it was really appreciated.

As the word spread, the number of men lined up every evening began to increase. Sometimes as many as 100 gathered. Feeding only five or six at a time, the Brothers worked four or five hours to feed all of them.

Brother de Paul talked to God and to his construction helpers and the answer came. "Let's convert the coal bin in the basement to a dining room. We don't need it for coal with our gas heat."

"But it's so dirty down there," one of the volunteers protested.

"Gather the workers and let's give it a try," Brother de Paul responded with characteristic optimism.

They scrubbed the sooty walls and covered them with knotty pine. Now they had a bright dining room that was large enough to serve 20 at a time.

Moving the men downstairs meant the second floor could be turned over to the Brothers. They used the little dining room for private meals, for visiting, for reading, for living. The volunteer workers kept on with their construction. They paneled the small chapel and kneelers and benches were paid for in monthly installments.

The men remodeled both Brothers' bedrooms and the founder continued to use his as his office for the first 17 years.

Chapter 9

In March of 1953 John Kondrak, Brother de Paul's father, decided it was time he checked on his son. Family and friends had asked him, "What was happening to Tommy?" He couldn't answer. Several times the past year he had sent Brother de Paul a dollar or two, but he hadn't visited him on Nicollet Island.

He felt uneasy as he walked into 26 East Hennepin. There were several men with dirty, worn and torn jackets sitting on the floor. They didn't pay any attention as John walked up the stairs to the small dining room. Brother de Paul greeted him, "Welcome to the House of Charity, Dad. This is Brother Martin." As John Kondrak shook Brother Martin's hand, he looked around at the bare furnishings. "Such a rat trap," he thought to himself. "How am I going to tell his family how he lives?" None of Brother's family liked his living in poverty and they couldn't understand his choosing this life.

Brother Martin served John a delicious dinner of fried herring and that appeased him a little. "At least you boys are eating well." He didn't come back for a long time.

In the summer of 1953, Brother de Paul left the House of Charity in the good hands of the seminarians from the St. Paul Seminary, to lead a bus load of pilgrims to the Grotto of the Redemption in West Bend, Iowa. It was a weekend excursion.

A tall, rather handsome man in his early forties, Mike Waren, originally from Wisconsin, was in the food line, having just been released from prison in California. "Thank you, thank you for the meal," he told one of the seminarians, "could I please stay here tonight?"

Mike stayed, and Monday morning when Brother de Paul needed a driver to pick up food from various donors, Mike did it. Within three weeks Mike was a part of the House of Charity. He helped serve the food, he prayed with them, and he was able to do almost any kind of work. The Brothers thought Mike was a prize boarder, but after a few months they realized he had a split personality — warm and captivating, but unpredictable.

One night at dinner, when Mike smothered his mashed potatoes with Brother Martin's delicious gravy, Brother Martin got upset with what he thought was piggishness. He cast an angry look at Mike, "Hey, you're going to get sick from all that rich gravy. That's too much!"

Mike didn't answer, but both Brothers knew he was seething inside. Even when the three of them went upstairs for their evening prayers the tension was there. Some angry words were exchanged and then Brother Martin announced, "I'm going to take a long walk to cool off."

While he was gone Mike told Brother de Paul that he was so angry with Brother Martin that he'd like to have killed him. This frightened Brother de Paul. The tension between these two men upset him.

Mike had been at the House of Charity about eight months when, on a Sunday afternoon in March, he came to Brother de Paul, "I've got to get out of here, Brother."

"Gee, Mike, do you want to talk about it?"

"No, I just have to go."

Brother de Paul found out later that Mike had an inkling of when his personality was going to change, and so he moved on. A year later, Brother de Paul got a letter from Mike. He was in Wisconsin State Hospital for treatment of his schizophrenic personality. The two men exchanged many letters, and several years later when Brother de Paul took a bus to visit Mike, the hospital superintendent thanked him for all the letters he'd written. "They meant so much to him. He's doing fantastic and he's going to be released soon."

Brother de Paul encouraged Mike. "Well, Mike, you've got a whole new future ahead of you. What are your plans?"

He didn't have any definite plans, but for a start, he visited his family in Superior. Brother de Paul didn't hear from Mike for several years. Then he heard that he was running a pizza parlor in Milwaukee. "Good for Mike," Brother thought.

In May, 1961 when Brother de Paul read the horror story in the newspaper, he couldn't believe it. Mike Waren had killed three people! His pizza parlor job had soured and he needed money. When he broke into a home in Springfield, Illinois to steal, the lady of the house and her four year old grand nephew were there. He killed them with a blunt instrument. The police, who were on the lookout for Mike said, "He was very friendly, warm, easy to talk to." That's the side of Mike that Brother knew.

A few days later, a fisherman was killed as he sat on the bank of the Nemadji River in Superior, Wisconsin. He had been hit with a stone that split his head open. Mike Waren's name was on a pair of blue gabardine slacks found with a bloody T-shirt in a railway work shack a couple of blocks away.

The FBI issued an all-points pickup for Mike, described as "a captivating, disarming personality." When they checked the state hospital, they found that Mike and Brother de Paul had corresponded; so they asked Brother to contact them if he heard from Mike.

A few nights later word went out that Mike was on Nicollet Island. Brother de Paul didn't sleep that night. He was afraid his co-workers might try to protect him from Mike and that might make him belligerent. Minnie Peronteau, one of the volunteers, knew him well as he picked up food many times at her house — she was so frightened by his horrible murders that Brother de Paul put her up in a hotel. But Mike was not on the island. It was a rumor. He had come as far as Cloquet, Minnesota, a short distance from Superior, when he was apprehended. "For all the bad things I've done, why don't you just hang me?" he suggested sullenly.

Brother de Paul visited Mike in prison. On one of his visits, Brother asked, "Mike, where were you really going?"

"To see you, Brother, but I'd never tell the FBI that. I might have endangered your name." After three murders, he was still sensitive.

Usually their conversations were very stinted and superficial. "How are you?" "My mother's sick." "I haven't had any visitors." or "Thanks for your letters."

During the fifth summer visit, Mike finally talked about the murders. When Brother de Paul arrived, Mike ran to him and hugged him — something he'd never done before. He told Brother about the horrors he was suffering. He couldn't sleep at night. How could God forgive him? He didn't try to defend his actions. He was just open about them. He continued to have a split personality, but most of the time he was a docile, likeable prisoner.

One time he set his cell on fire, but he didn't remember doing it. He asked to have his stamp collection put in a safety deposit box, just in case he started another fire. Mike had begun his collection when Brother de Paul had sent him some stamps from Rome. Now he was trading stamps all around the country by mail.

Mike Waren's tragic life disturbed Brother de Paul — his charming, outgoing warmth on the outside and a brewing volcano on the inside. He has kept in touch with Mike through the years, visiting him and keeping him in his prayers. Brother knew that this was the most he could do for this troubled man.

Chapter 10

Back to 1953. Many of the men who came to the House of Charity had a drinking problem. Some were alcoholics who had recently hit the skids, some were life long "winos," and some were drunks. As Brother de Paul would meet these men in the daily lineup, he would screen those who might cause trouble in the dining room. They kept a box of sandwiches near the door, and Brother would suggest they take some and be on their way.

But this bothered him. So when Bill Sinnott and Carl King came to see him to explain the function of Alcoholics Anonymous, Brother de Paul agreed, "That's just what we need here at the House of Charity. When can you get started?"

"This Sunday night, Brother. You can tell the men who come to eat here that any of them who has a drinking problem is invited to come to our first meeting."

And they came — six of them. Bill and Carl were pleased with even a small response and they decided to meet every Sunday, Tuesday and Thursday. When the House of Charity A.A. Group needed a spiritual advisor, Brother de Paul sought the help of the Reverend Forrest Richeson, an evangelical minister in the First Christian Church. Reverend Richeson had helped many alcoholics through the A.A. steps pertaining to "a Greater Power, God." Although he was not an alcoholic, he had worked with them since 1945.

Some of the men who came to the A.A. meetings lived and worked at the House of Charity while they were turning their lives around.

Brother de Paul will always remember Al, the gaunt 30 year old alcoholic who looked 50. "He had been drunk for ten years when he came to one of our A.A. meetings. He had tried, unsuccessfully, to 'dry up' many times, but this time was different. Al went through the Twelve Steps along with his friend, Peggy, also an alcoholic. They were married about a year later in the First Christian Church and had their reception at the House of Charity Dining Room."

Both Al and Peggy helped stabilize the weekly A.A. meetings and, later, they came to the ecumenical chapel services every Wednesday evening. Al worked for Minnesota Paints for 33 years, most of them as a recovering alcoholic in sobriety. Al and Peggy felt very close to Brother de Paul — as if he were their son.

Shortly after the House of Charity A.A. Group started, a wealthy man from a group in St. Paul came to visit. As Brother de Paul showed him the new dining room that had been the coal bin, the man noticed a kettle of beans on the stove, spoiling. "Where did these beans come from?" he asked as he poked his nose near the kettle.

"From the Telephone Company picnic."

"Why do you let them spoil in this heat?"

"I'm sorry, Mr. Preston. Just look at our small refrigerator." It had three legs and bricks held up the fourth corner. "We're desperate for more refrigeration."

"Brother, may I use your phone?"

"Sure, Mr. Preston, it's upstairs in my office."

While Mr. Preston was on the phone, Brother de Paul went up to the chapel for a quick and direct prayer. "Lord, take care of our refrigeration problem. I know You work through people like Mr. Preston. Amen."

When Mr. Preston came back, he announced, "If you could tell me the cost of a walk-in cooler, I'll buy one for you."

Brother was ecstatic as he went to Drawer B and took out plans for a walk-in cooler. Mr. Preston was so impressed, he bought it. The Brothers had been able to pick up more food donations when Father Hirman gave them a station wagon for a few dollars. Now they would have a place to keep the food cold.

The House of Charity was incorporated in July, 1953 with Father Leonard Hirman, Father Thomas Meagher, and Father Raymond Lucker, three priests who believed in its work, and five men who joined these "founding fathers" as the first Board of Directors: Charles Lappin, John Beckey, Charles Brown, Donald Novak and Robert Wilson. Ed Viehman of WCCO Radio fame became a Board member soon after. It was not easy to find people who were interested in working for the poor.

One of these founders, Charles Brown, had worked at the Catholic Boy Magazine with Charles Schultz, creator of the Peanuts comic strip. Mr. Schultz used his friend's name and features for Charlie Brown. Mr. Brown drew a sketch of the lineup of men waiting to be fed at the House of Charity. The drawing was used on the stationery for many years. He also helped feed the people on Christmas Day. It was fun for Brother de Paul to tell his friends, "The real Charlie Brown was dishing up dressing and gravy at the House of Charity today."

Ed Viehman was elected first President of the Board of Directors. As he conducted his first meeting, he said, "My prayer is that some day in the Twin Cities, whenever people have food, money, time, clothing or furniture to give away, they will think of the House of Charity." His prayer was answered through the years.

Chapter 11

Brother de Paul's friends had been his mainstay since he started this work. They had donated food, clothes, money, talent and time to his slowly developing House of Charity. As the old building was remodeled and the line of hungry men lengthened, more help was needed. Some of the men who stayed at the house helped with the cooking and serving, but that was not enough. The founder decided to invite more young men into his little community by advertising the works of the House of Charity in national magazines. "Wanted: young men deeply dedicated to serving the forgotten poor." A young man, 17-year old Mike Carter from California, read one of these ads in the Sacred Heart Messenger, wrote for more information, came to Minneapolis and joined the other two Brothers as Brother Anthony. Now the work load was a little lighter for each one in the community.

To ease his financial burden, Brother de Paul needed an auxiliary, especially for fund raising. With the fantastic accomplishment of Minnie Peronteau and Margaret Miller, two women he'd met on a pilgrimage to Chicago, a group of people from all parts of the city joined forces to form the Good Samaritan League. They held their first meeting in the fall of 1953, and Marge Johnson was elected president.

The League worked very hard having card parties, bunco parties, weekly bingo, outdoor fiestas, bake sales, style shows, rummage sales and benefit dinners. They have collected coupons and donated candy, soap and dish towels on a regular basis. It has been the backbone for any money-raising projects that Brother de Paul has been involved in. When he bought or remodeled or decorated the building, he never had the funds — only trust. His volunteers were always asking for donations, discounts or free services from carpenters, electricians, plumbers, doctors and printers.

Brother de Paul believed "God doesn't just send help. You have to go out and look for it."

Through all his years of mailing appeals, announcements and invitations, Brother has had free printing from Elwood Printing Company, Daily Printing Company and envelopes from Heinrich Envelope Company.

Thanksgiving 1953, Brother de Paul recounted the growth of the House of Charity since its inception, and he was grateful. He knew his 25¢ and his God were working. He thanked God for providing every person and everything he needed to feed and house the forgotten men, women and children of the city. He decided he would try to bring a bit of sunshine to the men and women in the city jail and the workhouse on Thanksgiving Day. By begging for cigarettes and candy, he was able to bring more than a handshake and smile to each of the inmates. He asked each one his name as he shook his hand and handed him a gift bag.

Chapter 12

The second Christmas, 1953, at the House of Charity was remembered as the Christmas in the coal bin.

"Last year we served six at a time. This year we can seat 20!" Brother de Paul reminded the helpers as they worked in the new dining room. But the tables had to be cleared, dishes and silver washed, tables reset, grace said and hot food served six times to take care of the 120 guests. They were served a very generous portion of turkey, dressing, potatoes and gravy, creamed cauliflower, cranberries, fruit, candy, cake, ice cream and coffee. There was a nativity scene on each of the two tables and Christmas hymns filled the air to help bring the true joy of Christmas to the men.

One young man was so touched by this special attention that he couldn't eat. Tears flooded his face. Not wanting to bother the House of Charity that evening, this young man was going to sleep in a boxcar. It was cold and he had no overcoat so, reluctantly, he returned to the House of Charity. The Brothers heard a commotion downstairs and Brother de Paul went down to investigate. He found the young man almost collapsed while two black men were trying to assist him. They put him into bed and gave him hot coffee to drink. Other men, who had come earlier for a night's shelter, made fun of him. They laughed at his unsuitable clothes for this time of the year. They ridiculed him until one of the blacks spoke up, "He's one of your white brothers, we're not, yet you're poking fun at him and we're helping him." There was dead silence. The next morning the young man was taken down to the clothing room in the basement where he picked out a warm outfit.

As the House of Charity grew, the bills grew. Brother de Paul had secured free use for the first few months from Mr. Rohne, the owner. After that, he paid $125 a month to buy the building for $11,500. Insurance premiums, interest, gas, electric and telephone charges brought the total to $300 per month; to be paid with an unstable income.

In January, 1954, they were flat broke, overdrawn at the bank and their creditors were pressing for payment.

Bea Baxter, a local TV personality and friend, arranged for Brother de Paul to make a last-ditch appeal on her afternoon television show. Brother told the viewers what he was doing at the House of Charity and why he needed the money.

The next morning, dollars started to arrive in the mail. As Brother de Paul opened one of the envelopes, he gasped, "$1000!" It was the largest donation the Brothers had ever received. The man who donated the money later confided that he first wrote the check for $250, and tore it up; wrote another for $500, tore it up; and finally wrote one for $1000 and put it in the mail. Once again, Brother de Paul knew that God would provide.

But it wasn't easy. Brother Martin had several bouts with pneumonia, and while he was in the hospital, Brother de Paul and Brother Anthony shared the extra work. Besides changing the beds, doing the laundry, cleaning, picking up free food, answering the phone, doing the bookkeeping, they had to cook and serve the meals. "We were too busy to be discouraged." Brother de Paul says, as he remembers those first years.

The advertising he had placed in national magazines began to bring in inquiries from young men who were looking for "hard work, a challenge, an austere existence." In 1954, Abe Camelia came from San Pedro, California and joined the new community to become Brother Stephen. A short time later, Dick Hulan, from Detroit, became Brother Francis. The brothers wore faded denim trousers and worn khaki shirts during the day, and the sacklike garb of St. Francis during their hours of devotion in the chapel. Their work at the House of Charity was not glamorous. In the summer they drove the station wagon all over southern Minnesota to pick corn, peas, beans and potatoes that were offered to them. The first year the Brothers took all the vegetables to the basement kitchen at Our Lady of Lourdes Church. Here they put them into cans and sealed them. When they went home they left the gas on under the non-automatic hot water tank and had to wake up the pastor in the middle of the night so it wouldn't blow up. The next year they froze the vegetables and rented a locker.

When the Brothers begged for food, they asked if they could come back the next week for more, and the next. They felt bold but they developed a weekly route of restaurants, stores, bakeries and produce markets to pick up free food. After begging all day, they had to come home and cook for the lineup of hungry men. By the time they cleaned up the kitchen and dining room and said their prayers, they were exhausted and ready for bed. Morning came early and sometimes they didn't even want to get up. They served breakfast at 6:30.

Brother Martin could make hot, tasty, nourishing meals out of anything — venison, antelope, herring, bear meat or the traditional beef, pork or chicken. Many times he would not tell the men what he was preparing for fear they wouldn't eat it.

By spring of 1954, the House of Charity had served over 50,000 meals in less than two years. There was so much work in begging for the food, picking it up, cooking and serving it and cleaning up afterwards that the Brothers decided they had to have live-in help. When Fred came to Brother de Paul and asked if he could stay with them and work for his room and board, he seemed to be an answer to a prayer. He was a clean cut, well-mannered 30 year old man who was a big help in the kitchen. When Brother de Paul found out he was married and had a daughter, he wondered why Fred wanted to stay at the House of Charity. He also wondered why Fred was so jumpy whenever a new face appeared in the dining room; his eyes showed he was terrified.

Finally, Fred told Brother de Paul that he was wanted by the police. "I cashed some "bum" checks and I was sentenced to a year in the workhouse, I couldn't stand it out there, and I ran away. I've been running for a couple of years."

"But, Fred, what about your wife and little girl?"

"Thats's why I left the workhouse. I was lonesome for them."

They talked from seven in the evening until two in the morning, and Fred finally agreed to turn himself in. He called the police and they picked him up. Brother de Paul visited Fred regularly in the workhouse and he tried to encourage him because he didn't adjust to his confinement. Fred worked in the bakery at the workhouse. After he served his year, he went back to his wife and child and got a good job as the assistant manager in a small department store. Successes like this helped the Founder in times of discouragement.

Chapter 13

When the House of Charity first opened, Father Leo Howley, from Northfield, Minnesota, wrote to Brother de Paul to tell him how happy he was to hear about the new project. A year later, Father Howley was called to the hospital in Northfield to visit George Meyers, a 74 year old man who had been found in a box car. His leg was broken and he'd been locked inside for several days.

"I was sure I was gonna die in there," George said later. "I pounded and I hollered and I even prayed that someone would find me. And finally they did."

When George's leg was healed, he had no place to go. He had been a real "knight of the road" — not a beggar, not a drunk. He had travelled from town to town and earned his way by doing odd jobs, especially cutting wood. He had never laid down his roots.

Father Howley called his friend in Minneapolis, Father Gerard Rowan, and asked about getting a place for George to live. "How about that 'House of Charity?'"

Father Rowan knew Brother de Paul would have a place for George with the dignity and love he would need — so he made arrangements for him to come to the House of Charity. George arrived July 1, 1954. Once more God showed his providence.

Even with hands crippled from arthritis, George became one of the workers. He helped make the beds; he became the "night watchman" if anyone got out of line; and he peeled the vegetables. It was difficult for him to walk but he struggled up the stairs to the chapel to join in the prayers every day. He trudged three blocks to Our Lady of Lourdes Church for mass every Sunday. It was painful going up the many steps at the church with his bum leg, but George was happy. He even went on retreats. He'd sit on the back porch peeling vegetables and he felt like he was king of the roost. Sometimes he'd be cantankerous, but everyone in the community loved him.

When, in 1956, the House of Charity opened its residence across the street, George had his own room. He was so proud. He continued to peel the potatoes, carrots, celery, and onions even though they had to be carried across the street.

One day, as George was trying to work with his knotty, arthritic fingers, Brother de Paul noticed he was crying. "Why, George, what's the matter?"

"I don't know if I can keep on peeling vegetables, Brother. My fingers hurt so much. I can't stay here if I don't work."

"George, you're going to stay here as long as we can take care of you. You're a part of our family."

When George had lived at the House of Charity for six years, he had a heart attack and was taken to the hospital. He told Brother de Paul, "I'm going in style, Brother. I've had the last rites of the church." Two months later he went to a rest home where he could get nursing care. The Brothers visited him, brought him food, sent him flowers and cards and kept him a part of the House of Charity family.

A year and a half later, George died. He was the first person to be "waked" in the House of Charity's little knotty pine chapel. A prayer service was held for the many people who knew him. Even Brother de Paul's mother, who found it hard to climb steps, insisted on coming. One plant bloomed near his casket. The next morning, Father Thomas O'Donnell, the pastor of Our Lady of Lourdes Church, had a high mass with requiem music for George.

In a non-evangelistic way, by showing him Christ's love in friendship, comfort and dignity, Brother de Paul felt that they had helped George come from the loneliness of a box car back to the strength of his faith.

Consuela Turner heard about "that House of Charity place that feeds the bums" and she was curious about it. One morning in July she drove to Nicollet Island and walked into 26 East Hennepin, expecting the worst. When she met Brother de Paul, she admitted, "I just had to see what kind of a place you're running here."

He took her on a tour through the dormitory, down to the dining room and upstairs to the chapel and meeting room. "You even have flowers in your chapel," she observed as they knelt for a short prayer.

"Yes, I have friends who bring in fresh flowers every week — mostly from funeral homes."

Consuela couldn't believe the cleanliness, the peacefulness, the orderliness. She liked what she saw.

While she was still there, Warden Douglas Riggs from Stillwater State Prison came for a visit. After he toured the House of Charity, he said, "It doesn't even smell like a mission."

Brother de Paul stopped him and Mrs. Turner, as he interjected, "because it is not a mission."

Warden Riggs called the House of Charity "an oasis in the desert of downtown Minneapolis."

"Why don't you buy the building next door?" Consuela asked. "You could cut a hole in the wall and make your dining room in there."

Brother de Paul shook his head, "Yeah, we've talked about it since the building is for sale. We still owe $8000 on this building though, so we'd never have the down payment on that one."

"How much is the down payment?" Consuela asked.

"$1,000."

"That's not so impossible. Give me a couple of months and I'll raise a thousand dollars for you."

Brother de Paul wasn't too convinced. But Consuela Turner was. She had no special fund raising skills, but she never missed an opportunity to beg. She'd stand on the steps of her church to collect a few dollars. She'd pull into a gas station and get 50¢ worth of gas for her car and a dollar donation for the House of Charity. She even exceeded her goal — she turned in $1060.

They bought the building at 24 East Hennepin. It had been used as a warehouse for 30 years, was unheated, had no plumbing or lights and needed a lot of work. Good Samaritan League volunteers came in to wash the filthy walls. Friends in northeast Minneapolis held a bingo party at Holy Cross Church and bought a stove.

In the midst of renovating, in September of '54, Brother de Paul was thrilled to have Dorothy Day visit the House of Charity. This famous writer and spiritual mother who had founded 32 Catholic Worker houses where the needy were given meals, lodging, love and spiritual counsel, had always been an inspiration to Brother de Paul. He had visited her in New York, and now she was here to speak at the House of Charity. Dorothy Day's greatest achievement was her ability to love, not only in her writings, but at close range.

Quote from Catholic Worker, 1941, by Dorothy Day: "It is not love in the abstract that counts. Men have loved a cause as they have loved a woman. Men have loved the brotherhood, the workers, the poor, the oppressed — but they have not loved man, they have not loved the least of these. They have not loved 'personally.' It is hard to love. It is the hardest thing in the world, naturally speaking . . . It is never the brother right next to us, but brothers in the abstract that are easy to love."

She lived in voluntary poverty, eating the same kind of vegetables, bread and soup that she served to the poor. As Stanley Vishnewski, her co-worker, said, "She put up with lice, dirty clothes, stale whiskey breaths, and unwashed bodies in close confines as she carried out Christ's command of love."

Dorothy Day spoke to a full house in the converted coal bin. Besides filling the seats, people were sitting on the stairs and standing along the walls. Someone took the front door off the hinges so the crowd could come in.

When Brother de Paul spoke to Miss Day later, he told her of the plans for the building next door. "But it's going very slowly. There's so much to be done."

"Don't worry, Brother," Dorothy assured him. "You will serve your first meal there before Christmas Day."

The Saturday after Thanksgiving in 1954 the House of Charity sponsored its first musical revue at the Stillwater State Prison. Brother de Paul had visited the men there, had seen the dreariness and ugliness of prison life and, in his compassion, had decided to bring them some music and laughter. Once again he begged for talent and for transportation for them. Thus was born the Sunshine Club. Under the direction of Ceil Trumble, a real estate saleswoman who had her finger on local talent, and the president of the Sunshine Club, 15 gifted youngsters, plus musicians, singers and dancers, combined their talents to present a variety show to an enthusiastic audience. A trio from the Musicians' Union on trumpet, accordion and piano furnished the accompaniment for the song and dance routines, baton twirling and Hawaiian and Spanish rhythms.

They brought cheers from the audience — "hardened men" — who were softened with the knowledge that these young people had shared Thanksgiving with them. In the December 2, 1954 edition of the Prison Mirror, each performer was mentioned. . . . "The men of Stillwater will talk a long time about the Thanksgiving Show. They will remember the moppets and young people who gave up their holiday to bring some light into an otherwise dreary day for "tough guys." They won't forget a dedicated young man who is called friend by more than a few unfortunates. Brother de Paul and the House of Charity will be remembered with warm thanks by every man who forgot, for awhile, that he wasn't where he'd have liked most to be on the 4th Thursday of November."

A lot of begging had to be done to finish the work at 24 East Hennepin. Mr. Lamb's plumbing company installed the drains and plumbing. They also donated the hot water heater and a plumber to hook it up. The Home Brand Company in St. Paul brought huge copper steam kettles. Miller Cafeteria gave a long steam table and a coffee maker. Egan Brothers Plumbing hooked up the steam. Friends donated more dishes and more silverware. Much of what the House of Charity needed, the House of Charity got. "It's God's providence," Brother de Paul kept saying. One woman gave a dishwasher, another gave 133 new serving trays.

Brother de Paul begged a record player so that Christmas carols drifted through the new dining room. Dorothy Day's prophecy came true. When she saw the new dining room, she called it "the Waldorf Astoria of feeding the poor in this country." Almost 200 men and women were fed that Christmas Day — 81 at a time. WCCO-TV featured the House of Charity on its newcast.

After the volunteers finished serving the guests, they were ready to sit down to eat their Christmas dinner. "Hey, folks, you're going to have to wait a half hour while I run a very important errand," Brother de Paul announced. He had remembered his old friend, Matt, whom he'd met when he worked with the blacks in south Minneapolis. Matt had been a minor league baseball player, but now he'd complained that no one ever visited him. Brother de Paul decided to take a turkey dinner with all the fixings and go wish Matt a merry Christmas.

He and his friend, Steve Sneider, a frequent Christmas volunteer, drove out to Matt's small hut. "You stay in the car, and I'll be back in 10 minutes," Brother de Paul promised.

As Brother walked in with the Christmas dinner, Matt turned the latch on the door. This surprised Brother de Paul a little, but he knew Matt was senile and didn't always think too clearly. "Merry Christmas, Matt. It's good to see you. I hope you'll enjoy this turkey and dressing and all — even pumpkin pie."

"That can wait, Brother," Matt said as he picked up a baby doll and held the small bottle and nipple up to its mouth. "The last time you were here you didn't care for my baby. Now sit down."

"But, Matt, your food —"

"The food can wait." He put his hand in the pocket of his jacket and pulled out a pistol. He pointed it at Brother de Paul, "I'm going to kill you!"

Brother felt his face blanch. "Why, oh why — I thought you were my friend."

"Not if you don't like my baby."

"But I do like your baby, Matt," Brother assured the old man. He chatted a few minutes, admiring the "baby," buying time. As Matt sat holding the gun on him, Brother tried diverting his attention. That didn't work. He tried apologizing for not caring for Matt's "baby." That didn't work either. Why didn't Steve rap on the door? It seemed many minutes had gone by. All the volunteers, including Steve's wife, Doris, would be waiting for them to get back so they could eat. The reason Brother went in alone was to make sure it would be a short visit.

Matt complained "No one comes to see me anymore."

"But everyone is so busy, Matt."

"They could still come to see me!" Matt cried, with desperation and loneliness in his eyes. Brother kept talking and asking Matt questions until he felt he was wearing him down. After almost an hour of terror, Brother asked with a trace of a smile, "You're not really going to shoot me, Matt, are you?"

Matt handed his gun to Brother de Paul. He sat down and cried, still holding his "baby." Brother unwrapped the foil on the turkey dinner, hugged Matt, wished him a Merry Christmas, unlatched the door and left.

When he got back to the car, he was ashen. Seeing him, Steve asked, "Whatever happened to you?"

"You won't believe what happened," and Brother told of the last hour. "Why didn't you come knocking on the door? You know all the volunteers are waiting."

"Why, I thought you were having such a good visit I just sat here listening to Christmas carols."

Brother de Paul fell apart and cried on the way back to the House of Charity, but when he got there, he couldn't tell his friends about his close brush with death. He ate very little — all he could remember was the cold revolver against his empty stomach in Matt's house.

He didn't abandon Matt. There were more visits, but no more threats. When Matt died, the priest from St. Elizabeth's Church called Brother de Paul. "He had told me you were his only friend. I guess he'll have to be buried in Potter's Field or else have his body donated to the University."

"No, not that, Father. We'll take care of Matt." Brother gathered the faithful few who rallied to this kind of loneliness and had a service at the mortuary. After a funeral mass at St. Elizabeth's Church the next morning, they buried him in a free plot in a nearby cemetery. Besides the priest, the mortician, Brother de Paul and eight volunteer pallbearers, no others came to the funeral. As Matt was lowered into the ground, Brother said to himself, "But for the grace of God, I wouldn't be here to bury you, Matt." Brother's heart swelled in gratitude that God placed one more person in his life to be befriended and loved until he was laid to rest.

Chapter 14

On the 9th day of January, 1955, as the Good Samaritan League met to plan its various fund raising schemes, a little lady with twinkling eyes and graying hair sat in on the meeting. Alice Codden was not a joiner. When she had met Rose Lutgen the previous Sunday after mass at the Basilica, she had bought a ticket for a House of Charity benefit. She had also listened to Rose tell about Brother de Paul, "this young man who works for the poor and needs our help. Won't you please join the Good Samaritan League?"

Alice had declined as politely as she could, "I never have joined any women's organizations. I'm really not interested."

Rose was insistent. "Our first meeting of the year is next Monday night. I'll call you Monday morning —"

"I'll think about it," Alice answered without much enthusiasm.

Monday morning, Rose called and Monday evening Alice attended her first meeting with the Good Samaritan League.

As the members talked about bringing cakes and cookies for a bake sale, children's clothing and toys for a rummage sale, and cooking the food for a Communion breakfast, Alice Codden thought to herself, "I don't like to cook or bake and I don't have any children's things. There must be something else I can do here."

When she thought about her 27 years as the manager of a credit office in Superior, Wisconsin, and now her office job in Minneapolis, she felt qualified to volunteer. "I'd be happy to help in the office," she offered meekly.

And she did. After an eight hour day in the office at Rossman's Model Laundry and Dry Cleaners, she'd hop the bus to the House of Charity on Nicollet Island. Brother de Paul always had things for her to do — mailing appeals and tickets, bookkeeping, and updating volunteer and donor lists. Soon she was coming in on weekends to catch up on the work.

After a year and a half of volunteering many, many hours, Brother de Paul asked Alice, "How about working for me full time for a salary? We need you here so much." When she didn't answer at once, he would leave the question written on her typewriter.

She had to think about the offer for a few weeks. It would mean a reduction in pay, but she would trust in God. A fellow volunteer's remarks didn't help. "Don't be too sure they'll keep you when the work is caught up. They'll say it's not the proper thing to have a woman on the staff with all the male community of young men and rehabilitation residents."

Even though it was daring and risky to quit her job, Alice was sold on Brother de Paul's work for the poor and downtrodden. She thought it would be a privilege to be a part of it, full time, and she began her vital, dedicated, all-giving role as his secretary. She was the only paid employee, and even though the bank balance has dipped to nothing at times, she has never missed a paycheck since she started working as Brother de Paul's secretary on April Fool's Day, April 1, 1957.

She shared Brother de Paul's office. She used a typewriter table for her desk. Although she was almost twice his age, Brother de Paul felt a comraderie with Alice that led him to share every joy and every sorrow with her. One of the residents dubbed her "Brother Alice."

In his Easter letter in 1955, Brother de Paul gave a sampling of the work the House of Charity was involved in:

"If you shared in the candy collecting, the smiling faces of the youngsters who receive the baskets will make your Easter happier . . . Shut-ins will receive Easter lilies. We don't have a ham in the house and 250 hungry people will be at our door on that day of rejoicing. Our total bills, the balance on both buildings, is $20,000. A rummage sale in late April will keep us going with our monthly bills.

"A Girl Scout troop from North Minneapolis had a canned goods shower for us as a result of our TV appeal. They all came down to see the House of Charity and they held their weekly meeting here. Every bit helps to keep us going. In March alone, we fed 7447 meals."

Besides a rummage sale in late April, Alice, the community and volunteers gave a birthday party for Brother de Paul in the new dining room with Bea Baxter from KSTP TV as the mistress of ceremonies.

In his thank-yous, Brother mentioned that a friend of Bea's gave the Brothers money to get haircuts for the party. He thanked Father Theodore Worm, OFM, and Father Rowan for "speaking so kindly about our work, those who had helped with the food and flowers for the party, for presenting my mother with a corsage and everyone for their fine gifts. The whole affair was a real encouragement for me personally, one that I can never forget."

The Good Samaritan League couldn't have a rummage sale every month, though, and the bills kept coming in. After several warnings from the company, a man came to turn off the electricity. "I'm sorry, Brother, but your bill is overdue and the time limit is up."

Not knowing what to do, Brother de Paul thought for a moment, then asked, "Would you give us fifteen minutes?"

"Sure, I'll wait fifteen minutes," the man replied.

Brother de Paul ushered his fellow Brothers — Francis, Anthony and Martin to the chapel where they prayed trustingly. Just as they finished, the doorbell rang. When they opened the door, a man handed them a check for $25.00, just what they needed to pay the electric bill.

The work went on with the new dining room — painting, wall-papering and putting in Venetian blinds. Mrs. B. Skjolsvik and her mission group donated screen doors and windows. Myrtle Kargel and Ruth McCoy gave a wrought iron image of St. Francis in memory of their parents.

The Good Samaritan League sponsored a housewarming for the newly opened dining hall and over 700 people came to see it. Two of the League members donated the lighting and statue of St. Anthony, the patron saint of bread for the poor, to whom the dining hall was dedicated. Hence, for many years, on the feast day of St. Anthony, June 13th, the centuries old Italian custom of the blessing of bread and lilies was held in the dining room.

With the larger dining room, the Brothers started to serve the meals at noon instead of the evening. The line of hungry men and women stretched for two blocks every noon and a neighboring businessman became very angry that they were blocking his doorway. "No one can come into my store," he complained to Brother de Paul, to the police and other neighbors.

After much dialogue, Brother de Paul yielded to the man's request not to block his entrance. Except for the very old, cripples, women and children who waited directly in front of the door, the people were told they had to stand where the bridge started, several hundred yards away. With a signal from one of the Brothers, the men could walk up to the dining room door. The bridge was open to the wind and snow in the winter, so some of the people would come in shivering and would hold a cup of coffee in both hands to get warm. In the summer, the heat reflected from the steel bridge was almost unbearable.

When a woman who vigorously opposed the feeding program asked Brother de Paul if he thought every person he fed deserved it, he said, "Ma'am, anyone who will stand out in 15° below zero weather on that icy bridge is hungry."

One day, Brother Martin was called across the street to the Commercial Hotel. Bill, a man in his 70's, lay on a dirty cot surrounded by chicken wire. His body was covered with urine and feces and lice. Brother Martin, who needed God's help to see His reflection in this decrepit man, cleaned him up and brought him some hot soup.

"Thank you, young man" the man's eyes showed his appreciation. After several visits where they talked about God, the man told Brother Martin, "I'd like to see a priest."

The man was given the last rites of the Church, and he died the next day.

Brother Francis found Agnes eating out of their garbage cans one day. She was munching a piece of dry bread she had retrieved. He asked, "Do you need help?"

"I have nothing. I have nobody," she told him. She was a thin, small white-haired lady in her 60's, with mental problems.

The Brothers found her a room across the street and she came to the dining hall to eat for several months. One day when she caused a disturbance with one of the other tenants, the police came to take her to the hospital for confinement. She refused to go until the police called Brother de Paul to come over to reassure her. He hugged Agnes and convinced her that it would be best if she went with the police. Later, when she was sent to the State Hospital in St. Peter, Minnesota, Brother de Paul visited her many times. He always found time for the lonely.

Chapter
15

For several years, Brother de Paul had spoken to church groups, political groups, youth and seniors about his work, and had received fantastic response. Now he had a new experience when the chaplain from Sandstone Prison wrote: "Please come up and speak to the prisoners on 'A Better Life.' We'll pay your train fare. You can come up in the morning and go back in the evening." Brother de Paul knew the names of some of the prisoners — they were the elite of the crime syndicate from all over the United States.

On the way up on the train, Brother was nervous. He had always had "butterflies" before speaking, but what could he say to these men? Most of them were imprisoned for serious crime.

He spoke from his heart, the only way this 26-year old could address this audience. He told them of God and how God treasured each person. He told them to look for beauty in life, even in prison. He gave them suggestions for coping day after day. He told them about his work at the House of Charity.

When he finished, the men gave him a standing ovation, and many of them came up to meet him. One of the men has responded to every House of Charity appeal letter since his release from prison.

On September 25, 1955, the House of Charity AA Group held its second anniversary banquet. The invitation cover had the words "But for the grace of God . . ." Inside was stapled the card listing the meeting nights, inviting anyone with a drinking problem to come to their meetings. "You will not be required to talk. There are no dues to pay. Come and listen." Then were listed the 12 steps of Alcoholics Anonymous.

At the banquet, Carl King introduced the members who had been sober long enough to receive one-year pins. Bill Sinnott told of the progress of the group since it had started two years earlier — some of its successes, some of its failures. Brother de Paul, never being satisfied with status quo, spoke of future goals for rehabilitation to help more people enjoy sobriety.

Another House of Charity group, the Sunshine Club, had done so much good bringing their musical revue to the prison and mental hospitals the previous year, they decided to put this year's show on for the general public. They called it the "All State Revue," and once again, Ceil Trumble put it together.

Alice Codden sent out notices and tickets to thousands of people telling them about the two-hour show that had some of the "best talent in the State of Minnesota." She promised singing, dancing, music and laughter.

Through Bill Sinnott, one of the founders of the AA Group, the Central Labor Union gave the performers free use of their auditorium.

The Sunshine Club thought they would make enough money to pay for buses to take the show to institutions for Thanksgiving. But because of timing or lack of interest, the turnout was small. Entertainers almost outnumbered the audience.

Brother de Paul had been feeling sick all day before the show, but he stayed through the evening, sweating it out. Pale and coughing, he had difficulty breathing. After the show, he went to Minneapolis General Hospital for a check-up.

After the examination, the doctor murmured, "Maybe you've got T.B. We'll get some x-rays," and he left the cubicle.

"T.B.!" Brother was in despair. The show was a flop, and now this. He and Brother Martin had spent many of their Sunday afternoons visiting patients at the T.B. Sanitarium in Glen Lake, and he knew how long they had to stay in bed. "Oh, God, please not T.B.!"

It was midnight, and he felt so alone. After about 10 minutes of self-pity, he thought of praying again. "Well, God, your will be done, but I don't understand what you're doing to me."

After an hour of being x-rayed, waiting to have them read, then x-rayed again, Brother de Paul paced the floor and was ready for the worst. Finally, the doctor came in and announced, "Good news, you have pneumonia. Go home and take this medicine and you'll get over it in about a week."

Brother de Paul was relieved to "just have pneumonia." It was the first of many times he had pneumonia. As he tossed and turned that night with pain in his chest and disappointment over the failure of the show, he thought, "we don't think big enough. I'd like to have a $50 dinner to raise money. I'll bet we could do it."

But the show went on. They performed at the Women's Reformatory in Shakopee, the state hospitals in Faribault, St. Peter and Cambridge, the St. Cloud Reformatory and the Men's Prison in Stillwater.

While Brother de Paul was at the prison on Thanksgiving Day, Brother Martin cooked and served the dinner. He left the dirty dishes to visit someone and the "boss" came back to the mess before he could clean it up. According to Brother de Paul, "Boy, did he catch hell!"

In his Fall letter to the benefactors of the House of Charity, Brother de Paul told about the early morning line-up. "Who would refuse a cup of coffee on these chilly mornings to our line of unfortunate men? — men who have been beaten down by circumstances, alcoholism, disasters, mental difficulties or a combination of these situations. Will we not follow Christ and take care of these least of our brothers, as He commanded us to do? What a pitiable sight, as winter nears, to see hungry men waiting outside at 5:30 in the morning for the little we can give them. Would you refuse them?"

For his Christmas appeal letter to thousands of his contributors, he compared the love and kindness of their family love, the warmth of their home and their clothing, the nourishing food on their table, and the luxury of having their own bed, to the men and women who would come to the House of Charity on Christmas Day. "Each one is without a relative or friend who cares, no home to call their own, without food, without love. Life has lost so much of its meaning for them. In many hearts and homes, 'there is no room for them.'"

Early on Christmas Eve, a young couple in their late 20's came to the House of Charity. The lady was sobbing and very pregnant. "What's the matter, my dear?" Brother de Paul asked.

"We've been to all the agencies, but they're closed. The workers are having their Christmas parties. We don't have a place to stay. We're hungry and I need some special medicine. A man on the street told us to come here."

Brother called a pharmacist and charged the medicine. He gave them each a bowl of soup, a sandwich and an apple. He found a room for them and invited them to come back the next day for a delicious Christmas dinner, and little holiday gifts.

That evening, all alone in the chapel, he read again the gospel of Luke, "There was no room for them in the inn." It took on special meaning.

When Brother de Paul discussed the dismal financial situation of the House of Charity with the Board of Directors, he suggested a fund raiser. He told them of the $50 dinner idea he had conceived the night he came home from the hospital. "Let's have a Charity Dinner. We can call it the Businessmens' Charity Dinner, because that's who we will ask for help."

"$50.00! Brother, that's a pile of money."

He convinced the Board of Directors, but many of his friends, volunteers and benefactors opposed the idea. It was tough selling expensive tickets to people who weren't familiar with the work of the House of Charity. But Brother de Paul wouldn't give up.

On Valentine's Day, February 14, 1956, in the Garden Ballroom of the Nicollet Hotel, 200 men and women paid $50 per couple and enjoyed a full evening of good food, from a half fried chicken, Parisienne potatoes to cherry cordial pie and good music. The main speaker was Emmet "Red" Ormsby — a famous big league baseball umpire. Brother de Paul announced that they were $800 short to pay off the mortgage for 26 East Hennepin. He looked around the hotel banquet room and four men ran up with $200 each. As he burned the mortgage at the party, he told the audience, "God certainly has blessed our work with so many generous people."

Finally, a special thanksgiving prayer was given by Father Theodore Worm, a Franciscan priest who had stopped at the House of Charity many times as he came from St. Paul to Minneapolis to see his doctor. He would ask, "Well, Brother, what did Daddy give you this week?"

Brother de Paul had looked surprised the first time he asked, "Daddy?"

"Yes, Brother," Father Worm had explained, "God is your father, but in the United States fathers are called dad or daddy."

That concept had brought God closer to the Brothers. He was not some far-off deity; he was right with them as a dad would be.

This charity dinner was such a success, it became an annual affair.

Chapter 16

Lent of 1956 was a painful, frightening time — a little bit of hell on earth.

As Brother de Paul tells it, "One of the Brothers had double pneumonia. He was anointed because he was near death, but after a few days he responded to the treatment. When he left the hospital, he stayed with friends who owned a restaurant on Glenwood Avenue North. He had to recuperate before he could return to the rigorous schedule at the House of Charity.

"He claims that one day as he left the apartment above the restaurant, he met the devil on the street."

"This Brother's return to the House of Charity was accompanied by many frightening demonstrations. Three of us slept in a small bedroom. He was in one bed, and another Brother and I were in the top and bottom of a bunk bed. In the middle of the night, the crucifix smashed to the floor scaring the daylights out of us. Then there was pounding on the walls and our beds began to move. We were terrified. I thought to myself, "Are we so exhausted we're seeing and hearing things?"

"The next morning I rushed to a clergy friend in St. Paul who had a responsible position in the church. I told him about the diabolic episode the night before.

"'Kondrak,' he said, 'I really don't know enough about being possessed by the devil, but before the rest of you are made to appear absolutely crazy, why don't you take him to a hospital for observation by professionals?'

"That afternoon when we took him to the hospital, he caused such a disturbance that the other patients had to be moved. He was isolated in a wing of the hospital — in a padded room, because he was thrown repeatedly across the room. Leather restraints popped off as he flew out of bed. When furniture started to move down the corridor, the hospital decided Brother better leave.

"He came back to the House of Charity where there were more disturbing manifestations. One noon the piano fell on him. It took six men to lift it off, but he wasn't hurt. I got in touch with the head of a monastery and they took him in reluctantly but he caused too much disruption there and some members of the monastery complained in fear. Back he came.

"Residents sleeping on the floor below us asked, "Why were you moving furniture all night? Who was pounding on the walls?" I had to tell a young man from Michigan who had just come to join us, but I hesitated for a long time before I told our volunteer secretary, Alice Codden, who worked nights in the office.

"After she heard some of the horrible noises we felt she would never return, but she did. We wondered how she could leave the dark building late at night and stand on the corner to wait for a bus. She was a brave woman.

"We approached each night with dread. A couple of priest friends came over each evening to pray with us and try to sustain us. They told the community and Alice that none of us had an obligation to stay with our work at the House of Charity, but no one left. The feeding and clothing and housing continued. These were very trying times, spiritually, emotionally and physically. Sometimes I wondered if this was mass hypnotism, but I knew better.

"Brother didn't seem to know what was going on within him. He seemed frightened, but he never said anything to us about what happened at night. One night his bed, mattress, blanket and floor underneath burned, but he wasn't touched. The firemen were sure he'd been smoking in bed, but he hadn't been.

"I feel in my heart that all these manifestations were done to destroy our work, but instead thay made us more determined to go on and grow. Don't think we were heroes. We were weak and we were frail. We shook in our boots and we looked at each other with horror in our eyes. We were three kids who were scared as hell. The power and strength and grace of God was with us, though, so we could continue. It took guts as this day-to-day thing threatened us, but we prayed like we never prayed before, knowing He would provide whatever we needed to go on.

"We didn't talk during the day about what was happening, but at night there'd be a knock on my door, and once again all hell would break loose. The other two Brothers would say, 'It's starting again for the night.' They were so tired — working all day and being disturbed all night. One night I gave them some money and told them to go out for a quiet dinner, a movie and a long walk — an unusual treat in our austere life.

"At the time this was happening, a friend suggested that we use radio and television to publicize it — 'It would put the House of Charity on the map,' he said.

"No, it wouldn't," I told him, "it would kill it." This was before people read or watched "The Exorcist." It wasn't the time to talk about it publicly.

"During Passion Week when Brother was in his private room — the three of us slept in the other room — I found him lying on the floor, unconscious. I couldn't wake him up, so I called Brother Francis. 'Get help — get it here fast!'

"It seemed a long time to me, but soon a short quick tempered Irish priest who had witnessed some of the diabolical events, came in. He had been so frightened by them that when he went home at night he had slept with the lights on. I briefed him on recent happenings. He put his hands on our associate and said with power and determination, 'In the name of Jesus Christ, I command you to leave this man.' Then he made the sign of the cross. It was a very heavy prayer. He was calling on Jesus Christ to put an end to this satanical conduct, to drive out the demoniac power surrounding our poor brother. There was no accusation against Brother — he was being used. After the priest said the prayer, Brother awoke and came out of his trance. After that, there was peace and serenity.

"Whether you, the reader, have the faith or not, whether you find things like this acceptable or not, you have just read what we experienced. It was all a living, breathing part of that Lent we lived through. It can be inspiring and encouraging, disillusioning or discouraging. React to it as you must or as you wish. Then just turn the page and go on reading."

In spite of the "diabolical" events taking place during Lent, the works of the House of Charity went on. Ceil Trumble took her live talent show to penal and mental institutions. The Sunshine Club spent $367.87 chartering buses to make this possible.

Easter was a busy time. Lilies that had been donated and used in the chapel on Holy Thursday had to be brought to shut-ins, candy baskets delivered to poor children, food baskets to needy families, and always the endless lines of people to be fed.

Chapter 17

On May 4, 1956 at 5:00 p.m., Brother de Paul left Wold Chamberlain Airport in Minneapolis for a pilgrimage to the Holy Land and to many of the shrines in Europe which were so precious to his spiritual life. Some of his benefactors made this trip possible, although most of them didn't know how much he needed to get away.

The original Fatima Group gave him a golden chalice, the vessel used to hold Christ's blood at Mass, to present for use at the Lady of Fatima Shrine as a memorial of the Fatima Peace Committee.

Brother de Paul met the parents of Francisco and Jacinto Marto, two of the children who reportedly witnessed the apparitions almost forty years before. They did not speak English, but they were happy to meet the young American and have their picture taken with him. They let him know that everyone takes their picture, but they never get to see them. Brother de Paul brought them a large photo on his next trip.

While Brother de Paul was in Konnersreuth, Bavaria, he visited the world famous mystic and stigmatist, Theresa Neumann, who reportedly lived without eating solid food and who had the stigmata, wounds that bled every Friday. When he saw her lily white skin, except for the wounds in her hands and forehead, he thought, "there's an aura of holiness about her, but still it's like meeting a living dead person."

In Assisi, Brother de Paul trudged the hills where St. Francis lived as a rich man's son, and later where he worked and begged for God's poor. He saw the frescoes depicting the saint's life and the crypt where Francis was buried.

Throughout his visit to Assisi, Brother de Paul felt a kinship with this man born almost 800 years ago. He was trying to do his work thousands of miles away with the poor in Minneapolis despite incredible obstacles, like Francis did.

When he walked the same streets as Jesus did in the Holy Land, Brother felt a closeness to Him that he had rarely experienced before. All the biblical stories became real to him. Israel had recently become an independent nation, and Brother de Paul was torn by the strife still going on between the Arabs and the Jews. Whenever the founder leads a pilgrimage to the Holy Land he has them carry a large wooden cross through the streets to get the "feel" of the first Good Friday . . . it is the highlight for all of his pilgrims.

For the last couple of years, the House of Charity had received such a large variety of clothes and household items that they couldn't use them all for the needy. Brother de Paul talked to two ambitious women about this and in September, 1956, Margaret Miller and Leona Weber opened the House of Bargains across the street at 25 East Hennepin, with second-hand merchandise spread out on cardtables and on the floor. They borrowed $100 to get it started and paid it back by the end of September. The group of volunteers who ran the House of Bargains became the Troubadors, after the medieval troubadors who, by their singing and dancing, brought joy and happiness to those who saw them. This group of men and women made great personal sacrifices to keep the House of Bargains open six days and two nights a week.

When the House of Charity bought two more buildings across the street, 21 and 23 East Hennepin Avenue, they moved the dormitory over there and remodeled the old one to make another dining room. Now they could feed 160 at a time. Storage space, a bread room and a vegetable room were added in the basement.

After remodeling the staff recreation room and public rest room facilities with volunteer help and materials, the House of Charity had an Open House. On Sunday, November 18, 1956, the volunteer hosts and hostesses were given a list of the "activities of the House of Charity":

Feeding the hungry people — also clothing many of them
Having beds for transients
Having an AA program for men and women alcoholics
Supplying complete needs of families and individual women
Shows taken to mental and penal institutions by Sunshine Club
Flowers taken to shut-ins and other sick people
Smile Fund — provides TV for patients who can't afford to rent one
Parties are given at rest homes
Lenten Devotions at the House of Charity each Sunday

Pilgrimages to various shrines in the Twin Cities and out of town

Paper mache' Bread Loaves placed in various business establishments with proceeds used to feed the poor

House of Bargains — second hand store with clothing, furniture, lamps, kitchen utensils, dishes, knickknacks, jewelry, etc.

Day of Recollection, a day of peace and quiet for the community, the residents, and benefactors on the first Sunday of every month, starting 1:00 p.m. and lasting til 5:00 p.m.

This was a heavy program, but it didn't include all the work behind the scenes. The food had to be collected, cooked and served, the clothing and all the merchandise in the House of Bargains had to be begged, picked up, cleaned and sorted. Not one cent was spent for food for the staff or the thousands of guests. Yes, guests. Brother de Paul felt that the people who came to eat were "down" and had suffered so much derogatory treatment from the jails, the missions, their families and society that the House of Charity had to give them some dignity, some warmth and some worth. The dining room had to be attractive, cheerful and an uplifting place. Rev. Leo Vetvick, a friend from the Covenant Church, remembered when Brother de Paul first showed him the dining room and each table had a vase of fresh flowers. There were huge bouquets all around the dining room. "Why, Brother? And where do you get them?"

Brother de Paul had a quick answer, "I think, if we can, we should add a little light and beauty to these mens' lives. We get the flowers from funerals." It hadn't been easy. He had made weekly calls to mortuaries before they had accepted the idea and had passed it on to surviving families. The food had to be tasty, hot and nourishing. It wasn't always possible to have a balanced diet, and sometimes the soup had to be watered a bit, but each person who came got something to eat.

Brother de Paul called himself "the most inveterate beggar." "I never stop begging because all that we have and all that we do is the result of someone's generosity. Our buildings, fixtures, food, kitchen — everything we have is a gift. It is through the generosity of people, sent to us by the providence of God, that we are able to help those in need."

The Creamette Company was one of the generous contributors. One day they donated 25,000 individual frozen macaroni and cheese pies. 25,000! The Brothers didn't know they could have rented freezer space, so after they filled their small freezer, they sent the rest to The Salvation Army, the Good Shepherd Sisters, the Little Sisters of the Poor, the New Hope Lutheran Center, Union Gospel Mission and the St. Paul Seminary. This was their first step in ecumenism. The Brothers, the residents and the volunteers got a little tired of macaroni and cheese twice a day. Sometimes

COLONIAL facade replaced two shabby store fronts at 24 and 26 East Hennepin Avenue on Nicollet Island, adding beauty and dignity to the free Dining Room. Second House of Charity.

the cook would take the pies out of the aluminum cup and put them on a plate with a little parsley to add variety.

Shortly after the macaroni and cheese windfall, part of the Christmas collection of funds was used to buy a walk-in freezer. What a boon that was to the feeding program!

As two or three hundred hungry men and women were lined up on East Hennepin Avenue that Christmas Day, several large fire trucks roared up and stopped near them. For a minute they wondered what was on fire. The firemen jumped off the trucks carrying cartons of cigarettes and bags of candy. They gave one or the other to every person in the line-up. It was the local fire department's bit of Christmas sharing.

At the second annual Businessmen's Charity Dinner, again at the Nicollet Hotel, Governor Orville Freeman presented a citation to Brother de Paul for "making great contributions to Minnesota and our entire nation through pioneering service in fields which are sometimes neglected or ignored." The dinner was another big financial success and Brother burned the mortgage on the second building.

The fund raising for the House of Charity went from the sublime to — well, collecting quarters for a new car. So far, there was enough for half a car. Agnes Vincent made regular donations of home-made soap, when buying soap was a luxury. The florists, Rosackers, Hermes and the Minnesota Florist Association donated over 100 lilies at Easter that volunteers like Jo Marek and various clergy brought to shut-ins in private homes and nursing homes. Brother de Paul and his helpers brought stuffed bunnies to needy children and to all the youngsters at Minneapolis General Hospital that Easter.

The Good Samaritan League kept busy with a Communion Breakfast and a fifth anniversary dinner. A couple of the women in the League had their private projects. Ethel Williams collected nylon stockings to make dolls for the fall bazaar. Consuela Turner collected Flame Room Coffee stickers, Hilex coupons and Rap-in-wax coupons. So far she was able to get a file cabinet for Brother de Paul's office and a three speed phonograph for the dining room.

After last years's big bash, Brother de Paul asked that no birthday party be given for him this year, 1957. Alice Codden and about 29 other active volunteers signed a letter asking that benefactors "show their friendship and appreciation to him with a birthday card, and an enclosure." Hundreds of cards arrived with "enclosures" of one to twenty dollars.

Chapter 18

On May 13, 1957, it was forty years since Mary, the Mother of God, had reportedly appeared to the children at Fatima. Brother de Paul sponsored a rosary service for world peace every Wednesday night at an outdoor Fatima Shrine at St. Leonard's Church in south Minneapolis. A huge billboard was erected across the street on the House of Charity property to commemorate this anniversary. It had taken a lot of talking and praying to get the billboard company to build it, and sell it to the House of Charity. When $750 was due on it, Brother de Paul didn't have any money. He turned it over to God and He came through again. A former Brother sent a check for $750. In large letters the message read: Have you recited your rosary today? Only prayer and penance will bring Peace as promised by Mary, the Mother of Christ, at Fatima, Portugal in 1917.

For many years, Brother de Paul conducted tours — to St. Paul, to Wisconsin, to Chicago. He called it the St. Francis Travel Service. As the tour guide, he always travelled free of charge. By bus, the group visited churches and shrines in Rudolph, Madison and Milwaukee, Wisconsin. When they went to Chicago, he took them to about 10 religious shrines around the city. It was a whirlwind tour to get them all in, plus a peek at the foreign markets on Maxwell Street, the Lincoln Zoo, a ride on the El, a ride along Michigan Boulevard, a visit to several museums and a trip up to the Board of Trade Observatory, the highest building in Chicago. All this from Friday to Monday. Brother de Paul felt that by combining a spiritual and a fun trip, he was making more friends for the House of Charity. They sang, they prayed, and they exchanged treats that each passenger brought. Before each trip, he would get the group together to tell them what they were going to see and the schedule they would keep. He had devised a way to unload the bus fairly and efficiently — alternating his directions, "right side out first," "left side out last."

The founder of this Travel Service was always organized and he always encouraged fun and fellowship. He always "bloomed," found great fulfillment when he made people happy, when he enriched their lives in any way. Many joined the auxiliaries and most became long time supporters of his work for the poor. What made the tours special was that he had great imagination and the travellers always saw places of great interest that were "off the beaten path" for most tourists. Although he spent intensive effort on promotion, it always appeared that it was easy because most of his tours were sold out way in advance. These tours gave Brother de Paul an opportunity to relax and "get away" as well as educate and enrich the lives of so many over the years.

Chapter 19

The House of Bargains second hand store was growing. By November, 1957, it was self supporting and soon after that it began to show a nice profit. Now the House of Bargains had its own 1½ ton truck which travelled all over the Twin Cities to pick up merchandise for resale. They advertised on the back doors of the truck: "We're loaded with bargains." Many of the people who came to eat at the Dining Room needed clothes, and with a note from one of the staff, they could pick out anything they needed. This way they found clothes that were the right size. When they lived in the same clothes day and night, they needed a new outfit quite often. Many poor families came to the store to buy furniture, kitchen utensils and clothes.

In his Christmas appeal letter of 1957, Brother de Paul challenged the recipient: "If God has blessed you with loved ones, a warm cozy home, sufficient clothing, friends, good meals and faith at Christmas time, show Him that you are grateful and ready to share with others who are sick, tired, discouraged, destitute, aimless and even desperate. . . . Will you not fill our outstretched hands begging for your assistance so that we might, in turn, give it to others in the name of the new-born Christ?"

Through the donations from this appeal letter, the House of Charity helped make Christmas a little merrier for over 1200 people — the men, shut-ins, mental patients, prison inmates, poor families and destitute children. One woman wrote, "May God bless you for remembering me. You were the only one who did."

They called their gift-giving project "Operation Christmas Cheer." In his visits to hospitals and correctional facilities, Brother de Paul had noticed that some of the inmates never received any gifts and this bothered him. Some of his workers suggested putting a box of fruit near the dining room door and each person could take an apple and an orange on his way out. "Never, never!" Brother de Paul objected. "Each person has to know we care about him." He, Alice and his volunteers very painstakingly made up individual plastic bags with candy, fruit, a Nativity scene and Christmas greetings which told each recipient, "This is for you." These gifts were taken to Minneapolis General Hospital, Minneapolis and St. Paul City Jails, Minneapolis and St. Paul Workhouses, Stillwater Prison, Shakopee Prison for Women, St. Cloud Reformatory, Willmar, Cambridge and Anoka State Hospitals.

For about the first five years of his work, Brother de Paul didn't allow any pictures to be taken, so there are not many photographs of the early years of the House of Charity. He didn't feel that having his picture taken would help his cause. He was trying to focus attention on his apostolate, not on himself.

People who came to the House of Charity to visit were told in no uncertain terms, "No pictures!" Alice Codden went along with this restriction as long as Brother de Paul felt so strongly about it. Many times during benefits or on tours, as people were ready to shoot, she would speak up, "Please don't take any pictures."

Most people couldn't understand Brother's reluctance and they thought he was just stubborn.

By 1958 he had a change of heart about being photographed, "Perhaps it will help the House of Charity to see a picture of its founder. Brother de Paul preferred to be photographed in action with people, his guests in the dining room, his workers or shut-ins.

When Alice saw the first few pictures of him, she said, "You're much warmer inside than you look on these pictures, Brother. Why don't you smile? You have a warm, beautiful smile." But the founder has never liked to be photographed.

Chapter 20

1858 - 1958. It had been 100 years since the Virgin Mary appeared to Bernadette Soubirous in Lourdes, France and since then, millions of pilgrims had visited the grotto every year. Brother de Paul wanted to make a pilgrimage there during this centennial year, but because he never got a salary, he had to devise a way to travel cheaply. He worked out a deal with the American Express World Travel Service where he would get all his expenses paid as a tour leader.

A 21-day air pilgrimage to Europe took Brother de Paul and 24 sturdy travelers to Lisbon, Portugal with a one-day excursion to Fatima on May 13th, the anniversary of Mary's appearance there. From Lisbon they went to Madrid and on to Lourdes.

The group's three days in Lourdes, France were spent at masses in the Basilica, in the procession of the Blessed Sacrament followed by the blessing of the sick. In the evening, the torchlight procession, in which they chanted the "Ave Maria" in concert with thousands of pilgrims carrying lighted tapers, was followed by the rosary and Benediction in the Grotto.

They left Lourdes by train to spend a day in Nice and then on to Rome by air. Whenever Brother took a group on a tour, he tried to make it personal for each traveler. He knew that Howard and Eleanor Hommes were celebrating their silver wedding anniversary while on the trip; so he made arrangements through Msgr. Rudolph Bandas in St. Paul for a private mass in St. Peter's Basilica. All 24 pilgrims were gathered around the altar at the tomb of Pope Pius X — everyone except Howard and Eleanor knew why. When the Papal Secretary, Bishop Van Lierde came in to say the mass and two women pinned flowers on the couple, they were surprised and delighted. The two women had gone to many floral shops in Rome asking for a corsage and boutonniere but no one understood what they wanted. They settled for a spray of flowers.

Howard and Eleanor were so touched by everyone's thoughtfulness that they had a champagne party for them in their hotel room that evening.

Brother de Paul wanted his group to have an audience with Pope Pius XII, but he hadn't been able to arrange it beforehand. He spent several days making contacts in Rome and then he met Cardinal Leger who was leading a large group from Canada. He told him about wanting an audience. After a lot of persuading, the Cardinal accepted Brother de Paul's suggestion. "Have our people join your group and pretend they're all French Canadians." They did, and soon they were all enjoying a Papal audience.

Father Raymond Dierman from St. Louis, Missouri, who was with Brother de Paul's group, passed his hat around to take up a collection for the Pope. He got $100. Then he remembered that the Catholic Digest had recently published an article telling about "The Works of Mercy on Skid Row — The House of Charity." "Let's put a copy of the Catholic Digest article in with the money," he suggested. Brother de Paul had the article in his brief case. They put it and the money in an envelope and Father Dierman worked his way up to Pope Pius XII and handed it to him. Many months later, when Brother de Paul was meeting with Archbishop Brady in St. Paul, he discovered that the Pope had read the article. The Archbishop showed anger as he told Brother, "I've been a Bishop for 19 years and I've never been called on the carpet in Rome before. When I presented my annual report last month, one of the Cardinals asked, "Why haven't you mentioned the House of Charity? The Holy Father read about it in the Catholic Digest." Brother and his community knew they were not officially a part of the Institutional Church.

The pilgrimage continued on to Paris, then to London and home.

Chapter 21

Early in 1958, Bishop Bernard Topel of Spokane, Washington, contacted Brother de Paul about the possibility of starting a House of Charity in Spokane. The Brothers prayed about the request, they struggled and even fought over it. It was a tough decision, and they decided once again they'd rely on God's providence.

Brother Martin went out to Spokane as the "advance man," and he found a lot of support from both Catholics and Protestants. Brothers Edward, Pius and Francis joined him for the hard work ahead. They renovated an apartment house and opened it for needy families who needed temporary housing. According to the Inland Register, the diocesan newspaper, "Each apartment has its own kitchen facilities so that families may prepare their own meals with food given to them by the hard-working volunteers at the new House of Charity.

"Jobless family men who bring their families to the House of Charity will be able to devote their full time to job hunting; men and their families will be welcome to stay, not only until a job is found, but until the first pay check brings independence."

When the House of Charity for family living was only a few months old, the Brothers began working on an old hotel that they converted to a home for men similar to the one in Minneapolis. They had a lot of work to do before they could open their doors and their dining room to the poor, the lonely, the alcoholics and the transients in Spokane.

Bishop Topel gave them much support. He rolled up his clerical sleeves on Christmas Day and helped serve the dinner. He made the front page, wearing his white apron and he wondered how his fellow bishops would feel when they saw the newspaper. On Easter Sunday, he said the first mass in the barely completed chapel, and officiated at the corner-stone laying. The four Brothers served as altar boys as 60 people — homeless men, members of the Spokane Good Samaritan League and other friends of the House of Charity — participated in the mass. Bishop Topel had recently moved out of the official Bishop's mansion into a small $4,000 hut, planted his own garden, made fish soup and drove an old jalopy. He related to the people the House of Charity served.

The Brothers worked hard setting up their feeding and housing programs and they got a lot of cooperation from the Spokane business people. Just as in Minneapolis, they begged, they cooked, they served and they cleaned the kitchen and dining room. They had ample food donated so they could feed three to four hundred people every day.

Through the next two years, the Spokane House of Charity suffered the same pains as Minneapolis. There was the same drinking, fighting, lice, filth and stealing among the men. There were too few Brothers to do all the work and eventually all but Brother Martin either quit or went back to Minneapolis. Brother Martin broke off from the Minneapolis community and continued to run the Spokane House of Charity with the help of local volunteers for about a year. The building was torn down eventually and a smaller House of Charity was opened downtown. The St. Vincent de Paul Society operates it today.

Since 1950, the Minneapolis City Government had been trying to change the face of the Skid Row area. By 1954, the Gateway Park at the entrance to Nicollet Island had its streetcar passenger shelter and public comfort station taken out and was filled with trees and flowers. There was a four foot high fence to keep out the loafers.

In 1956, a dozen businessmen were told to move to make way for a new Federal Courts Building. A 12-million dollar federal grant had been approved to begin demolition. By 1958, a block of buildings was torn down to make room for a new library.

In 1959, 50 of the 200 Skid Row properties were purchased and condemned, and in 1960, wrecking crews went through lower Nicollet and Hennepin Avenues and along Washington Avenue taking down another dozen bars, cafes, hotels and missions. Some of these businesses moved to other locations, some just died.

The old men wandered among these ruins wondering where to turn next. The flophouses were all gone, most of the missions were gone. Some of the men moved to other parts of Minneapolis, some to downtown St. Paul, and some of the transients took a freight ride to other parts of the country. The Minneapolis Housing and Redevelopment Authority helped many of the men get resettled within a radius of one mile from their former lodgings.

Meanwhile the people who lived on Nicollet Island felt the impact of the death of Skid Row. Would they be next? A group of parents met in 1957 to start building up their neighborhood. A census revealed that 34 permanent families with 80 children lived on the island besides a number of single and elderly men at the Salvation Army and the House of Charity.

The parents established a playground for their children; they organized a general community clean-up; they established family fun nights in the DeLaSalle High School gym, and they set up a polio clinic on the island.

This community family spirit touched Brother de Paul and the other Brothers because they knew each of the families and men who lived in the flats on the island. They didn't want the demolition of Skid Row to include their beloved Nicollet Island.

Chapter 22

It was noon when Father Veit from Whittemore, Iowa looked out the window at the Great Northern Depot. He was waiting to take a train back home. When he saw a long line of men stretching over the bridge, he asked the porter, "What is that line of men doing?"

"Theye're waiting to be fed."

"Is there a big restaurant across the bridge?"

"No, Sir. They feed people who are hungry."

"Do they charge?"

"No charge."

"I can't believe it," the priest went off shaking his head.

When Father Veit got back to Iowa, he decided he wanted to include this feeding place in his will, but he didn't know the name of it. He wrote, "To the charitable institution that feeds the men who line up on the bridge across from the Great Northern Depot."

After the priest died, the probate judge wrote to a judge in Minneapolis to find out what this "charitable institution" was. "No question about it," the Minneapolis judge concluded, "it was the House of Charity."

Because this priest, who had never met Brother de Paul, liked the concept of feeding the hungry for free, the House of Charity received $3,000. Once again, God multiplied the 25¢ Brother had when he started. That line of people was good advertising to all those riding by on the buses or in cars, and all the passengers coming or going to the Great Northern Depot. It told of the great work done by the House of Charity.

There was never any discrimination shown because of race, sex, color, religion or the lack of it, handicaps or age. They did limit their sleeping quarters for men only. If women needed a place to sleep, the House of

Charity paid for them in a nearby hotel. It was a warm summer evening when Brother de Paul saw the fire engine down the alley. He realized a car was burning and he knew that an Indian couple lived in that abandoned car. That was their home, where they could stay together. As he approached the car, the husband who was seriously burned over a great part of his body was being put in an ambulance. The wife was burned beyond recognition, and she was dead. The policeman turned to Brother de Paul and asked, "What do you want to do with her?"

Brother was taken aback. "Well, I do know her; she and her husband have eaten at our place. I know her name is Marie Bearallten. If she has no family, we'll be happy to bury her."

Brother called the Kapala Funeral Home and they took care of 33-year old Marie with no charge. A friend donated a casket and a cemetery plot at St. Anthony Cemetery was found. Father James Namie, a Maronite priest, conducted a short service at the cemetery; in the middle of it, the manager of the cemetery came up and said, "You can't bury this person here without paying for the plot. She doesn't belong to any parish." This made Brother de Paul angry, and the small group of people who always shared in these lonely events, were appalled. The House of Charity barely had enough to exist on, but he gritted his teeth and told the manager, "We'll pay. Just bill us."

It wasn't that easy. The man went to his office to make a few phone calls — checking on Brother de Paul's credit! After some time, Marie was lowered into the ground.

That same summer, Jim Williams, the president of the Creamette Company called Brother de Paul. "I have a real favor to ask you."

"What is it, Mr. Williams?"

"I want to come to the House of Charity and volunteer in your dining room, if I may, five days a week for a month."

"You — you — in our —?" Brother stammered.

"Yes, I want to do some real work, and I want to be anonymous. I don't want anyone to know who I am. No one."

"But, why, Mr. Williams?"

"Well, Brother, I feel I need to get out of this office, away from the company. I want to work for people in real poverty."

Mr. Williams washed dishes, cleaned refrigerators and scrubbed floors for a couple of months. "Boy, this is the real work of God," he told Brother after the first week.

It was great for him and for the House of Charity. Brother de Paul was impressed to see a man of wealth and influence happy to be on his knees scrubbing a floor or polishing a copper kettle until it glowed.

The breakfast menu included Wheaties for weeks after the House of Charity received the following letter:

July 9, 1958

Dear Sir:

This is to notify you that your organization is being shipped a free case of New Wheaties compliments of the Wheaties Sports Federation and Ed Sadowski of the Minneapolis Millers baseball team.

General Mills, through its Wheaties Sports Federation, is awarding a free case of Wheaties to every Minneapolis player hitting a home run at Metropolitan Stadium this American Association baseball season.

All the players are donating their Wheaties to a local charity organization.

Ed Sadowski hit his home run June 29, 1958, aganist the Louisville baseball team, and has designated your charity as the beneficiary of the case of Wheaties.

Sincerely,

Jerry Brennan
Executive Secretary

There were many surprises for the community. A farmer gave them a carload of sweet corn, another a truckload of rutabagas. When 10,000 pounds of potatoes were brought to the House of Charity from Barnesville, Minnesota by the Minneapolis Jaycees, they had them boiled, baked, fried and au gratin — potatoes and more potatoes. The Minneapolis Tribune's front page story began: "1 Potato, 2 Potato, 3 Potato, 4." Altogether, 40,000 pounds of potatoes were shared with the Union Gospel Mission, Salvation Army, the Good Shepherd Home and the Mission Farm.

Since the first year that the Fatima Group was started, and later the House of Charity, Brother de Paul had reserved the Sunday after Thanksgiving to show his appreciation to the many who had helped him during the year. He called it the "Smorgasbord Internationale" — a Christmas Appreciation dinner.

He brought the benefactors together to get to know each other; to form a bond of fellowship and friendship. It was not a benefit, there was no charge, no collection or no pledge, but the foods came from everyone who was invited! Each person could choose which foreign dish they would bring. There was Italian ravioli, lasagna, and pizza, French ragou and tourtiere, Hungarian goulash, Spanish rice, Polish krupi, galomki and sausage, Mexican tamales, Chinese chop suey, Irish stew, Hawaiian delight, German sauerkraut, and American chicken supreme. In addition to the authentic foreign dishes, there were unusual foods, such as: bees and ants in chocolate, sparrow wings, fried grasshoppers, snails and pickled octopus. During the program, each person was asked to share a little about themselves. The Founder loved being a host at social events.

Brother de Paul wrote his annual Christmas letter to the thousands on his mailing list and a separate letter to local labor unions and to A.A. members. To the latter he wrote:

"Fellow sufferers of alcoholism, who still live daily under its tyrannical, unsatiable desires will just exist through this Christmas season. They will think of the meaning of Christmas, remember former Christmases and drown their sorrows with alcohol.

"We take care of many, many of them each day throughout the year; at Christmas time we will be trying to make the House of Charity a real home or haven for them.

"Because you know what it is to enjoy sobriety, and because the season will be one of significance for you, you can show your gratitude by making a sacrifice to help others who still see that "hopeless hope" in that bottle."

By January 23, 1959, contributions of one dollar to twenty-five from individuals and five dollars to sixty from union locals and A.A. squads brought in $2,851.50.

There were so many demands on this money. There was constant remodeling and repairing required by city and state inspectors — the buildings were almost 100 years old. Earlier in the fall, Brother de Paul had run into Sally De Vay, a wiry lady in the upper sixties, who had operated the nursery school at St. Leonard's Church. She told Brother de Paul of her dream. "You take care of homeless men but what happens to homeless women? I'd like to open a home for them. Can you give me any help to get started?"

Brother de Paul remembered his early days with the House of Charity and he knew how Sally felt. "Let me think about it, Sally," he said with a smile, "I may come up with some help for you." And he did. The original house that Helen Drellack let him use at 1506 Second Street Northeast now belonged to the House of Charity. It needed rewiring and redecorating, but when he offered it to Sally, she was ecstatic.

"We'll pray, that I can get an electrician to do the wiring, and with a little more help we can make it a comfortable home." She begged for furniture, food, clothing and money — and she got it. Brother de Paul shared food from the House of Charity for over a year and at Christmas time, gave them a stereo and television set.

Wayside House, as it was called, took care of 41 women the first two months it was in operation. They had been sent there by Travelers' Aid, the Parole Board and Alcoholics Anonymous. There was such a need for refuge that the four bedroom home soon was outgrown, and the Wayside House moved to a larger building. Following Brother de Paul's example, Sally organized the Wayside House Womens' Auxiliary to help with the work. Admission to Wayside House later was limited to alcoholic women only —

and is still operating. Sally turned to new projects. Shortly after the Brothers opened the House of Charity in Spokane, Sally took the train to the west coast — she had another dream. She started St. Margaret's Hall for destitute women in Spokane. When she came back to Minneapolis she ran a Coffee House at St. Stephen's Church. Here she met many Indian families and was so interested in their welfare that she volunteered as a VISTA worker with the Indians in Wisconsin. She was almost deaf and 79!

Chapter 23

When Pope John XXIII was installed in October, 1958, he immediately shared his stately life with the poor and imprisoned. Brother de Paul had met Pope Pius XII, but Pope John was his kind of man — especially when he said, "Charity is the Apex of all." Shortly after his pontificate began, he personally visited Regina Coeli prison in Rome.

But to carry on with the work of the House of Charity in Minneapolis where they were feeding over 300 a day, and in Spokane, over 400, they needed more help — more workers. After an article about the House of Charity was published in the Catholic Digest, many young men from all over the United States and Canada responded. From 150 inquiries, 11 candidates were chosen. Some of the others were not ready to dedicate their lives to this work. Brother de Paul kept in touch with them, though, by writing several letters each year. In the spring of 1959, he wrote:

"Today was Sunday and all the Brothers took a nice drive in the country. The weather is beautiful here this time of the year; in southern Minnesota spring is about ready to be really "sprung." All around us we see GOD's law being carried out so perfectly in nature. It gets me to wonder about how many of us do exactly what GOD wants us to do. When HE calls, we are much too reluctant to answer promptly and generously. What beauty there is in nature and in man submitting to HIS will!

"I didn't mean to get so serious, but it's what I've been thinking. Because you wrote to me shows that you had a desire to serve GOD as a brother; it is well to act promptly when HIS grace comes as so many times this grace will not come again and a vocation may be lost forever.

"Last June we opened, and now have in full swing, our House of Charity in Spokane, Washington; Bishop Topel blessed our new chapel there on Easter morning and offered the first Mass. It is really beautiful and what a privilege for us to have CHRIST present in our house! We are planning another house for our community to take charge of this fall, and we face the very same problem all communities do: shortage of good vocations.

"You may think that this apostolate is very difficult at times; well, it is. But doing it for CHRIST and HIS poor make it a joy and actually a wonderful privilege. If you are worried about being worthy, don't. None of us is really worthy of serving CHRIST, but when HE calls we respond with gratitude. Our young community has such terrific possibilities of helping our fellow man and glorifying GOD that sometimes the thought overwhelms me. With our daily work, Divine Office, Rosary, etc. comes the graces each day to sanctify ourselves and perfect ourselves in virtue. Right now we are feeding over 300 a day in Minneapolis and over 400 a day in Spokane in addition to our other works of mercy. GOD certainly must be pleased. Yet we know this is only the beginning, for we have calls for our community in many places. Each vocation enables us to move another step forward.

"May I ask for your prayers as I need them badly; rest assured that my prayers will be offered for your vocation which should be a most precious thing to you. May we meet often in exchange of prayers! (Please send the enclosed card to let me know of your interest.)

GOD love you!

Brother de Paul

Thank you."

The men who became brothers had to be an inspiration to the people off the streets or in jails. The name "Brother" was accepted by these people, not as a religious community, but as a brother in Christ.

Because Brother Anthony had taken a leave of absence after several bouts of illness, and because Brothers Martin, Francis, Pius and Edward were still busy in Spokane, the Minneapolis House needed these new recruits. They became Brothers Joseph, Michael, Benedict, Stephen, Leo and William. Some of the men left before the end of their training — some left before it started. One day as Brother de Paul was scrubbing the lobby, a young man walked in carrying a suitcase. He carefully stepped over the scrub pail and around Brother to go up to the second floor office. Alice Codden, the secretary, was in her office when the young fellow walked in. "Are you in charge here?" he asked.

"No, I'm not," she explained, "The head of the House of Charity is in the lobby. You must've passed him on your way up. Is there something I can do for you?"

"No, thank you," he answered emphatically. "I don't want any part of this life if the head one has to scrub the floor." He took his suitcase and left.

Most of the brothers were under twenty years old when they came, and Brother de Paul felt they needed some discipline. These young men helped with every facet of the work — feeding, cleaning, laundry, chapel services and alcoholic rehabilitation.

Brother de Paul was a very strict director with his confreres. Schedules were followed religiously — no alibis. No one was allowed to be late for prayers. Each one had his assigned duties, and he was expected to perform them impeccably. There was no smoking, no regular spending money, and clothing and possessions were limited. Besides the community and Alice, there were daily volunteers who came in to help with the telephone, the mailings, with seasonal projects and with the House of Bargains. Then, usually, eight or ten alcoholic men lived at the House of Charity where they were given a lot of love and encouragement. Many of them were able to remain sober and return to their jobs and family. Often it took a year of care and prayer to do this. During the year, or years in some cases, these men were given jobs in the kitchen, the dining room, the warehouse, or on the truck. If they held jobs outside the House of Charity, they paid a minimal rent — fifteen to thirty dollars a month.

Shortly after the two houses were established in Spokane, Brother de Paul had another request. Archbishop Duke and Coadjutor Archbishop Johnson of Vancouver, British Columbia, asked the community to take over the Catholic Charities Hostel. The hostel had been built above the Chancery Office from funds collected from Catholics in the 1956-57 University, College and Welfare Appeal. Now they needed someone to run the program for feeding and housing the destitute of Vancouver.

Brother de Paul and Brother Joseph went out to British Columbia to get the program started. They, like their forebear, Francis of Assisi, Brother Joseph and later Brother Benedict began to beg for the poor. They needed bedding, blankets, pillows, hand towels, dish towels, dishes, pots and pans, and canned food. The founder stressed that they didn't want people to give more, they wanted more people to give. At their first "open house" they asked each person who came to bring a gift of food.

The hostel could accommodate 120 residents, or as Brother de Paul called them, "guests," and the two kitchens could feed 150 men daily. They planned to work with Alcoholics Anonymous, rehabilitating the men and women who came to them, just as they were doing in Minneapolis and Spokane. The people of Vancouver were very responsive to the brothers, and they opened the hostel with a mass in the chapel, celebrated by Archbishop Johnson. One of the honored guests at this Mass was "Brother Alice." Her friends at the House of Charity had given her a trip to Spokane and Vancouver as a birthday present.

This was not a good time for the Community, though. With three houses of charity to supervise, Brother de Paul would leave Minneapolis, fly to Spokane, do his visiting and fly on to Vancouver that same night. He'd do more reviewing and supervising the next day, then fly back to

Minneapolis. He admitted, "It was such a hectic pace, it nearly brought me to a nervous breakdown."

On November 4, 1959, he wrote to Archbishop Duke: "Since our arrival in Vancouver six weeks ago, three candidates and one young brother have left our community. This has placed an enormous burden on the rest of us. There has also been some difficulty with the U.S. Selective Service about having draft age men assigned outside the United States. I know this can be ironed out. Brother Joseph has returned here for that purpose.

"Our council met and decided it would be unwise and imprudent to allow one brother, Brother Benedict, to remain alone in Vancouver for any length of time. Thus, we are reassigning him temporarily to our Spokane House of Charity. ---

"In the meantime, may we humbly suggest that other men operate the hostel. ---

"This has indeed been crushing to us, but we know it is one of the crosses that God allows and gives to new communities. It has been decided that three brothers in our large operation here in Minneapolis is not enough. Eventually, it would be disastrous to their health and well being.

"May we beg for prayers for increased and persevering vocations to this apostolate for His poor, and that soon we may re-enter Vancouver when God wills that we have sufficient staff."

The House of Charity never had sufficient staff to return there, but the Vancouver Hostel is still in operation above the Chancery Office, run by the St. Vincent de Paul Society.

Chapter 24

Easter has always been a time of renewal for Brother de Paul — Christ's resurrection has given him hope to go on with his work. On Holy Thursday, with the altar bedecked with lilies, the residents of the house came to the chapel for a service. A resident read from scripture, Sylvia Little, or one of the many singers who came to the House of Charity, sang "Were You There?" and then Brother de Paul put on a white apron, took a pitcher of water, a bowl and a towel and went around the chapel washing the feet of each man: residents, volunteers, guests and clergy. He kissed each foot reverently. He felt that just as Christ washed the feet of the apostles, he should serve his men in the same way.

EASTER, TIME OF HOPE . . . The founder and a guest look over colored egg and the tray of food in the Food Centre at meal time.

The Easter lilies were distributed to shut-ins on Good Friday and Holy Saturday by priests, ministers and volunteers. On Easter morning the men gathered on the porch where there was a sunrise service with prayers, alleluia hymns and readings. At noon, about 400 people, the poor, the lonely, the winos, enjoyed a delicious ham or chicken dinner. Each place had a small basket of colored Easter eggs.

Toward evening, the Resurrection Service started with a trumpet blare as a live lamb was brought into the chapel — the Paschal Lamb of God. After the reading of the gospel story of the Resurrection, the trumpets again blared, balloons were broken, and everyone sang, "Allelujah." It was always a tremendous Easter celebration.

The House of Charity's Alcoholics Anonymous Group 26 had both men and women receiving their 5-year pins, their 4-year pins, their 1-year pin, their 90-day pin — even their 30-day pin. With counseling, with love, with food, and with a place to stay, many alcoholics were turning their lives around to sobriety. Meetings were still held every Tuesday, Thursday and Sunday.

They began to publish an A.A. Newsletter with Brother Joseph as the editor. After spending his day begging food, driving the truck and supervising the laundry, Brother Joseph used his evening recreation time to do this. Besides telling about the "Pin Parties," the week-end retreats, and the 12 steps, they had a column called "Around the Table." It had quotes from members' discussions pertinent to alcoholics. A few of the quotes:

"A.A. is not for the guy that needs it, but for the guy that wants it."

"We have to divorce ourselves from former habits, places of temptation and so-called drinking friends."

"Remember, it isn't the drink I can't have, but the one I don't want that keeps me sober."

"An Alcoholic is never more than one drink away from a drunk."

"The simplest way to refuse a drink is to say, 'No, thanks.'"

The group read about the Irish alcoholic, Matt Talbot, who was a confirmed drinker at age fifteen. He would pawn his clothes for the price of a drink. When he was 28, he gave up his job in order to have more time for liquor. Then, on a Saturday in 1884, he came home sober, took the pledge, first for three months, then for a longer period, and finally, for life. He worked as a builder's laborer, but also as a laborer for the Master Builder. He lived on $2.00 a week and gave away $13.00 to anyone in need — a fellow workman, a child, or someone in a far-off mission in China. The members of Group 26 were so impressed with Matt's sobriety, they named their meeting room and their library after him.

During the summer of 1959, Brother de Paul attended Yale University School of Alcoholism. His expenses were paid by A.A. friends. Rev. Richeson, the first clergyman in the upper midwest to take this course, had recommended it to him. It was a very concentrated course. For five and a half days a week, Brother de Paul made an accurate, scientific and very solid study of alcoholism. The physical, emotional and spiritual aspects of Alcoholics Anonymous which he had witnessed in Minneapolis for over five years became more real to him. When he returned to Minneapolis, he felt he had a better understanding of and better rapport with the alcoholics who were being rehabilitated at the House of Charity.

Chapter 25

When the demolition of Skid Row started in the mid-fifties, Brother de Paul opposed uprooting all the people who had spent much of their lives in this area. The Housing and Redevelopment Authority reported that before the renewal, 17% of the people in Skid Row lived in standard, acceptable living quarters. After renewal, the figure rose to 83%. When he saw that many of them found better homes a short distance away, and that tearing down the old sooty buildings and putting up new ones like the Minneapolis Public Library, the Federal Courts Building, and the Northwestern Life Insurance building would improve the appearance of the area, he began to go along with it. He felt it was better to spread the former Skid Row inhabitants into five or six small areas rather than have them all in one big lower loop concentration.

One of the largest of the missions in the world, Union City Mission, was destined to go. The St. James Hotel, which was operated by Union City Mission, the Minnesota Hotel, the large Janney, Semple, Hill warehouse and the much-loved Metropolitan Building all went under the wreckers' blow. The latter was demolished despite concerted efforts and thousands of petitions to save this landmark.

But some things in the Gateway area didn't change. The poor, the newly unemployed, or those who didn't want to work, the wandering soul, or the down and out drunk still gathered in their old haunts, but instead of a flop-house or cheap saloon, they sat in the Minneapolis Public Library. Some of them read the newspapers, some of them sat in the hall and panhandled.

An anonymous letter published in the Summer 1974 issue of Common Ground, a quarterly magazine concerned with Twin City neighborhood history, reveals a woman's personal backward view of the vanished Gateway. She called the men "bums" but Brother de Paul never tolerated the word. He thought it added to their degradation.

"I was not a bum, I held a job. I was not a hooker. It just happened that I was in love with a man who worked in one of the cafes on Skid Row. That's how I got to know the people.

"We were a united group. Once you were in, you were always protected and safe, as long as you lived by the rules.

"As for the bums, I knew many of them. Some were old men who had lost their wives, their children drifted off, and their loneliness drew them to the Avenue . . . Many were dirty, I agree, as they slept in box cars, on park benches, covered with newspapers to keep them warm. They enjoyed a friendly 'Hello' or just the thought that someone cared enough to say a few words to them. I always felt they were some mother's son."

These "Mothers' sons" were the people who were described in a WCCO-TV telecast on Christmas Day 1960.

"Their Christmas morning would start with hunger pangs if it were not for services provided by such as the House of Charity at 26 East Hennepin Avenue — and operated by the Franciscan Brothers.

"Generally, about 30 men turn out for breakfast, which is served from 5:30 to 6:00 a.m. The breakfast includes rolls or donuts, coffee, some type of fruit and most of the time, there is cereal. Since the food is donated, there is always the chance that the Brothers will run out of a certain item — presently, they are out of cereal and it will stay off the menu until someone donates enough to replenish their supplies.

"The line for the noon meal usually numbers close to 200, but for Christmas dinner, today, the dining room will be filled half a dozen times until nearly 500 people have been served."

"Besides the meal, each person was given a small gift — candy, cigarettes, a calendar and some hankies all wrapped and tied."

The television broadcast didn't include the behind-the-scenes bedlam early Christmas morning. Ray, a fantastic cook, had prepared most of the dinner the day before, but on Christmas Eve he went out and got drunk. The community tried to have him "sleep it off" fast, but 500 people were waiting. All the amateurs served the dinner.

Earlier in the week, individually wrapped packages were sent to the residents of state mental hospitals, state penal institutions, people in local nursing homes, to needy families, to patients at Minneapolis General Hospital and to anyone whom they heard about who was lonely. Alice Codden, Brother de Paul's right hand in this Christmas assembly of gifts, and her helpers worked day and night, sometimes until 1:00 a.m. She made sure that each package was wrapped and tied with a large bow and a lot of love.

The House of Charity had developed a list of shut-ins, starting back when the brothers spent their Sunday afternoons visiting the patients at Glen Lake T.B. Sanatorium. They still spent their Sundays visiting the sick and shut-ins. The list grew to include shut-ins from across the United States and Canada. Mary Ellen Kelly, a well-known shut-in from Iowa, who wrote "With the Dawn Rejoicing," supplied the founder with the names. They had as many as 1200 names, and they sent each one a Christmas card designed by Brother de Paul. Throughout the year he signed and sent birthday cards to each one on the list. Sometimes these were the only cards the shut-ins received. Many mothers and fathers who couldn't afford gifts for their children were invited to the House of Charity to choose books or toys to take home for their young ones' Christmas. The lonely men were given free greeting cards and postage and were encouraged to send cards to other lonely friends or long forgotten relatives.

Christmas was a special time at the House of Charity — a busy and a happy time.

One of the most inspiring highlights of Christmas Eve was and still is the annual traditional candlelight ceremony. The House was completely darkened, except for a few night lights. Brother de Paul explained to the men, to benefactors, to nuns from nearby convents and friends how the world was dark with sin until Jesus, the Light of the World, came. "Our lighting ceremony symbolizes what took place on that first Christmas — we, as His followers, will give light to a darkened world." Then, as they all sang, each man went to the altar to light his candle, and then slowly proceeded to various parts of the house, singing, "Oh, Come All Ye Faithful." When they returned to the chapel, one of the men read the Gospel of Luke, telling about the birth of Jesus. To insure an inter-faith approach, Brother de Paul usually invited a Protestant Minister to give a short message, and then they sang Christmas carols with the nuns leading.

One of the men, 85-year old Holger With, had tears in his eyes as he lighted his candle and said, "This is my best Christmas ever!"

Chapter 26

In the early sixties, George Holland, a parole and placement officer in the Department of Corrections and a friend from DeLaSalle High School days, approached Brother de Paul and asked if the House of Charity could take in a fellow who was getting out of prison on parole. He had absolutely no place to go.

Brother responded, as he most often did when there was a human need, "Sure, bring him in."

There were several more of these "special cases" who were brought to the House of Charity. Both George and Brother de Paul agreed that these men should have separate quarters but could work, eat, pray and share recreation with the transients and residents.

"What we need," George explained one day at lunch, "is a program for these men. Some place where they could get used to their new freedom and get help finding a job. Do you want to get into this kind of service — a half-way house?"

Brother de Paul was interested, but all the rest of the community thought he was asking for trouble. Many of the volunteers and staff vigorously opposed the idea, too, and protested in strong terms. He had the support of his faithful secretary, Alice, and Dr. Spano, President of the Board of Directors. Brother de Paul thought the Half-way House would fit into what the House of Charity was supposed to do at that time, to be there if there was a real need. It would be a challenge, and he loved challenges.

On Thanksgiving Eve, 1962, he called the news media to a press conference at 10:00 a.m. at Ferrara's Restaurant. He thought people would be in a kind and giving mood before the holiday, and be more receptive to his announcement. "Our halfway house for parolees will be called Roncalli

House, in honor of Guiseppe Roncalli, Pope John XXIII, who has shown his love for prisoners. Shortly after he became pope he visited the Regina Coeli Prison in Rome. The prisoners loved him, too."

As Roncalli House was established, the men were given their own reception room, coffee shop, and sleeping quarters. There were as many as 25 men at a time, each going through a jittery readjustment to the outside world. Just getting out on the street with traffic was a frightening experience or doing things without a bell ringing was a challenge to the men.

With the opening of Roncalli House, there were more expenses, so naturally, Brother de Paul had to have another fund raiser. Although he was 100% Polish, he had a lot of Irish friends who were benefactors, volunteers and even men in the lineup. Why not combine a St. Patrick's Day Party with making money for the parolees' program?

Brother de Paul's good friend, Father Paul Dudley (later Bishop) of Annunciation Church offered his big auditorium. Marie Fagerstrom, who Brother discovered had artistic talent, and her girls from the Good Samaritan League outdid themselves with the decorating. The hall looked like "a wee bit of the old sod."

Father Michael McDonough, the master of ceremonies at the first dinner, drew a standing ovation when he said, "Brother de Paul is a one-man order, a one-man Peace Corps and a one-man circus!"

Although the first St. Patrick's Day dinner earmarked for Roncalli House was a flop financially, Brother de Paul continued this fun fund raiser. When he didn't pinpoint the halfway house, the response was better.

In the next fourteen years every Irish speaker in the area was tapped, and many Irish singers and dancers performed. You didn't have to be Irish, though. Cyril Paul, from Jamaica, the Bednarz family, Lutheran seminarians, Franciscan Friars, the Gateway Singers, Sylvia Little, Pat Donnelly, and many others added a touch of lilt with their songs. An attraction was a $100 prize, and the drawing was done by Miss Minneapolis or Miss Minnesota Teenager.

In 1965, the big St. Patrick's Day blizzard almost closed down the party, but not completely. There were 300 reservations and 86 sturdy souls showed up. Brig. and Mrs. John Troutt, friends in the Salvation Army, surprised Brother de Paul by coming. He came through the blizzard with a cast on his leg. The speaker, Episcopalian Father T. N. Libby, who founded halfway houses in Canada, arrived at the airport and was told to get on the next plane out before all planes would be grounded; and the emcee, D. J. Leary, had to leave early for his television show. There were huge kettles of chicken untouched, so the next day the men at the Food Centre had a full course "Irish" dinner.

Since 1977, the letters asking for help still go out before St. Patrick's Day, but there's no party. Brother de Paul said, "Sure and begorrah, 'tis much easier this way!"

Brother de Paul went to the Stillwater State Prison to parole hearings and had interviews three mornings a week with men who were prospects for Roncalli Halfway House. Since they couldn't take all who wanted to come, Brother de Paul had to decide whom they would take. Once they were accepted, he was the only person who knew their crime. Confidentiality was part of the dignity shown these men. No one knew a murderer from a burglar, and there were many "lifers" who had committed murder or manslaughter who came to Roncalli House. This was the first halfway house to accept them. A new law had been passed that allowed "lifers" to get out after serving 25-30 years.

There were rules for the parolee. He had to stay at least two weeks, he had to have a job before he left, he was not allowed out overnight, he had to do his assigned job in the kitchen, the House of Bargains, going out with the truck to pick up merchandise, or do office work. He could leave in the evening and all day Sunday, but he had to be in by a certain hour. Every Monday evening he had to attend a meeting with other parolees and the staff. They discussed their progress, or lack of it, in adjusting, their job potential, and their personal problems. They were a support group for each other.

Roncalli had both outstanding successes and dismal failures. Bob was one of the latter. He was handsome, refined and cooperative. After his two-week adjustment program, he found a job and left. Several months later, he came back to the House of Charity to see Brother de Paul.

"Brother, I lost my job, and I have to have another one right away. It's urgent!"

"Well, Bob, I can't get you a job today."

"I'm desperate, Brother. I'm going to rob a bank." He sounded as though he meant it, but Brother de Paul couldn't put his finger on a job for him that very day.

That evening, Bob was on television. The news bulletin said that after the robbery he was caught several blocks from the Savings and Loan bank — wearing a red hunting coat.

Brother was awestruck. "He must've wanted to be caught — otherwise he would've worn subdued colors. My guess is, he couldn't make it out in the world. He needed the security of prison."

A few days after Christmas, Brother de Paul received a card from Bob. "As I lie here in jail on Christmas Eve, I hear the chimes from the tower clock. All I can think of is that little chapel you have there on the island. There was so much love and happiness there. I will never forget any of you. It helped me get through Christmas knowing you folks were praying in that chapel."

"We didn't rehabilitate Bob," Brother de Paul said sadly, "but we touched him and showed him God's love."

Frank J. had been in prison for 33 years. He had killed someone when he'd been drunk on the farm. After that many years, he was very institutionalized — he'd be up early in the morning, work hard all day, listen to the 10 o'clock news, and be asleep by 10:16 p.m. Every day. He was tall and strong, and Brother de Paul put him to work in the kitchen. The cook was a tiny woman, but Frank was afraid of her. He had never talked to a woman in 33 years. She was afraid of him, too, at first, but they became good friends. He worked tirelessly and had a big grin that melted everyone he met.

After three months, Brother de Paul urged Frank to get a job. "But I like it here at Rocalli House." He had gone out only twice since he came.

"Frank, this is a halfway house — half the way to where you're going."

He moved out, but only next door. He came over every morning and worked in the warehouse for a free lunch.

"Frank, you've got to get a job." Brother de Paul reminded him.

When his parole officer found him a job in the restaurant at the airport, he was as happy as a young boy.

One day Frank told Brother de Paul, "I've got a couple thousand dollars I saved in prison. When I die, I want it to go to the House of Charity." But there was no rush to make a will.

Several months later, Brother de Paul got a call early in the morning. Frank had been robbed and killed as he walked home from work that night. Everyone at Roncalli House and the House of Charity was heartsick. "Frank had just begun to live," they lamented, "and then he had such a cruel death." Brother considered Frank one of their successes. At his funeral at Holy Cross Church, Brother reminded the handful of mourners, "We were his only family." His savings went to the state.

Joe was neither a complete success nor a complete failure — maybe a little of each. He was a very talented artist and shared his creative skills with anyone who had a project for him. He made a manger scene for the House of Bargains and Christmas place cards for the tables. He worked in maintenance and kept the rooms spotless. Why was a charming and talented man like Joe in prison? Unarmed robbery. This was the third time he'd been imprisoned. Joe loved to gamble. Harold's in Reno was his paradise, and someday he thought he'd make it big.

One morning, about a month after Christmas, Brother de Paul was across the street at 23 East Hennepin, supervising remodeling of the recreation room for the residents. All of a sudden, Alice Codden came in the door. This was unusual because normally she only came over late in the afternoon to pray in the chapel. Brother de Paul looked at her as if to say, "What are you doing over here?"

Immediately, Alice knew she'd been taken. Joe had been in her office while she had been getting the bank deposits ready and he'd told her,

"Brother de Paul wants to see you right away, Miss Codden." When she rushed back to her office, both Joe and the money were gone — $566.88.

Brother heard later that Joe had lost all the money at Harold's in Reno and was picked up in California for another crime. He was back in prison.

Several months later, Joe wrote:

"I have no explanation for what I did to you except that it was stupidity in the highest form. I was very happy with the way I was treated and all of the others went out of their way to make life pleasant for me in every respect. I am so ashamed of myself and nothing that I could do in the future would rectify the wrong that I have committed against you and my God. I only ask that you remember me for the little good that I was able to do for you and your wonderful organization and in some way you can find the forgiveness in your heart for what I did. I know I violated the law of trust that you and Alice gave me and this is what hurts me the most of all for there was no reason for me to commit this violation.

"Tell Judge McDonough that I am truly sorry for letting him down as he also had great plans for me and not to judge me too harshly for my deed. Oh, how I wish that I could relive that one foolish moment of the day I jeopardized my whole future, the fine Christian life that I was surrounded with and the wonderful people that I came into contact with."

When Brother de Paul let Joe know that he'd forgiven him, Joe wanted to come back to Minnesota to "make amends" to Brother and to the Roncalli House. He asked if he could be paroled to Brother de Paul. The first time he went before the Parole Board his petition was denied, but Joe wasn't discouraged. He wrote: "This extra year has been good to me. It has given me deeper insight into the problems that have plagued me these many years. It has been a painful experience because to look at myself honestly has been humiliating. Facing up to the terrible deeds I have been doing is not a pleasant task. How I must have hurt you and the others after all the faith you all placed in me.

"I still want to come back and make amends. I know that to erase the wrong is impossible, but I want to try to restore your faith in me."

Joe did make amends. When he came from California, he brought over $200 that he had saved by selling articles he made in the hobby shop. When he worked again at the House of Charity, he earned very little money, but he kept repaying until the $566.88 was erased — both from the books and from peoples' minds.

Bill was one of the parolees who used both Houses — Roncalli Halfway House helped him return to the world, and the Talbot House helped him reach sobriety. Two years later he was told he had terminal cancer of the mouth and neck. When he went through the A.A. Step 8, "Make a list of all persons we had harmed and become willing to make amends to them all," Bill decided he had to go out to visit his sister in California. He had dropped her out of his life twenty years ago, and he didn't know how much time he had left to "make amends."

They spent three weeks together — filling in the gaps of these many years, and re-establishing their love. While Bill was in California, he wrote to Brother de Paul:

"Brother, when I worked on my A.A. fourth step inventory, it scared me and discouraged me — I didn't see how such a dissolute life as I had led could ever be atoned for but, somehow, there was a spark of something that told me it was better to give it a try and fail than to give up and continue on fruitlessly. I had had no spiritual or religious rearing in the home except that my mother was continually admonishing me with a fearful, vengeful and punishing God who would wreak horrendous injuries upon me if I did not do this or if I did do that. It took a lot of doing, a lot of meditation and a lot of praying — I didn't know how to pray then — to come to know that God is Love. From that first morning, when I asked for His guidance through the day to be sober, industrious and honest and to do nothing to or say anything about anyone that I would resent having them do to or say about me and then thanking Him at night for seeing me through the day, I began to find tranquility and peace of mind. I discovered that in living this way one day at a time, following my God-given conscience, that I could have no yesterdays to regret nor any tomorrows to fear. I have failed often, perhaps everyday, in that my selfishness has prevented me from extending a helping hand and giving positive aid to my fellow men. It has always been so with me. I believe my sins of omission far outweigh my sins of commission, though I committed an untold number of them, too. That is my problem now, I have put off so long letting my sister know the facts about my health simply because I was so selfish that I didn't want or wouldn't let anything mar what could be our last get-together. I could just jump on a bus with my return trip ticket and let her know afterward, but that would be the most cruel of all, so I know I'll find the courage to tell her before I leave and hope and pray that she takes it in stride and doesn't despise me for it.

"Before I get on with the immediate practical problem I face, I have to tell you of something I did just a year ago, before I had any idea it might come about so soon. I had read so much and was expounded to by an M.D. acquaintance about the dire need for cadavers in medical research, science and aid to education that I decided, in view of the fact that I had contributed so little to the betterment of mankind, here was an opportunity to be of some service, so I bequeathed my body to the University of Minnesota. At the same time, I bequeathed my eyes to the Lions Eye Bank. I do not know whether this is contrary to any religious concepts or tenets, I do know that we need doctors and that doctors cannot be made without cadavers."

It was Brother de Paul's belief that beer incomes with champagne appetites put many men in prison. Then, when they were serving their time, prisons augmented this materialistic thinking. Rehabilitation meant having an impressive job, living in an exclusive area and driving a new car. When they got out in the world, the men lacked the references and skills necessary for this kind of success.

"The material things are not important to us here," Brother de Paul emphasized. "I think the way we live and operate gives parolees a different perspective about what makes a man a success."

"One thing they all know," he continued, "even in the caverns of the most crusty hearts of them, is that we are here at Roncalli House to help them — again and again."

In about eight years, there were 400 parolees who lived at Roncalli Halfway House and according to Will Turnbladh, the Commissioner of Corrections, they were more successful than the general parolee population. "Many of the men placed at the Roncalli Halfway House would not have been able to succeed on parole without the reinforcement, the individual guidance, and the favorable surroundings."

When Roncalli Halfway House was started, it was the seventh such house in the world. It was a new concept in rehabilitating parolees as they re-entered the real world. Meanwhile, other halfway houses were opened. Brother de Paul wondered if the people in this new type of work shouldn't organize into a group to share their ideas and techniques. He contacted as many halfway house directors as he could find in the United States and Canada and solicited their help and interest in establishing the International Halfway House Association. There was not a lot of enthusiasm but Brother went against the odds and called them to a conference in Chicago.

In 1964 he and Dr. Spano, who was still the President of the Board of the House of Charity, flew to Chicago for this first meeting. Before the conference, the two men had visited halfway houses in six states, a whirlwind, exhausting trip. Directors or representatives from about 35 halfway houses came to share their ideas and experiences and to learn from each other. Brother de Paul, again a founder, was elected the first President of the International Halfway House Association. He and Dr. Spano were thrilled to host the fledgling second annual conference of the organization in Minneapolis. The program included a look at types of halfway houses, a panel discussion by former prisoners looking at halfway houses, problems of community acceptance, maintaining personal and professional staff, and a report on the first 100 men of a halfway house in Newark.

Brother de Paul was proud to conduct a tour of Roncalli House to show what had developed in its two and a half years of operation. They had given love, security and self-confidence to hundreds of parolees. The warmth, cleanliness and physical attraction of the residence was evident. "It was all worth it."

Chapter 27

As a pioneer, Brother de Paul encouraged ecumenism even before the word was known from Vatican II, which brought many changes in the church. He called it fellowship. He believed that every person had the right to his own beliefs, that his beliefs should be respected, and he should be given the chance to share them. Brother de Paul had come a long way from his Polish, "Nordeast" Catholic youth.

The majority of the men who came to the House of Charity were not Catholic, so Brother became informed about many Christian, Jewish, Orthodox and even Moslem and Buddhist religions. Much of his support came from Protestant and Jewish benefactors. As one Catholic lady who headed a charity drive for the poor of Appalachia told him, "If we had to depend entirely on Catholics to support us, we'd have closed down years ago. It's unfortunate that many Catholics are not tuned in to the corporal works of mercy — that part of Christianity that is helping people."

From the first years he was on Nicollet Island, Brother de Paul had depended upon his other Jewish friends, besides Jesus. He called them "the Three Wise Men." Art Lapidus, from Hy's Men's Store, kept Brother de Paul in shoes, sox, shirts and trousers when he started his work on the island. He was a staunch supporter for the House of Charity in the East Hennepin Avenue Businessmen's Club. At one meeting, when the business men were very upset about the House of Charity drawing people from all over the city, Art was the only one who stood up and spoke in favor of Brother de Paul and his work.

Joe Fliegel, a retired prize fighter, was Brother de Paul's volunteer prison coordinator. He drove Brother de Paul to the prisons to interview potential parolees, and when they were released he brought them to Roncalli

House. Sometimes he even took them to his own home. Joe would visit the men who were to be released from prison, find out what kind of work they could do, and most of the time, he would have a job waiting for them when they got out. When the House of Charity was in a financial "pinch" at Christmas, Joe raised $1,000 among his friends.

The third Wise Man was Ed Rose of Rose Confections. For the first few years, Alice and the volunteers spent days and nights getting the Christmas candy ready for each person in hospitals, jails, and mental institutions. Each bag had to be filled, weighed, and tied. When Ed Rose offered Brother de Paul a good price on the candy, plus bringing it in all bagged, the whole Christmas Gift Project crew was relieved. Each year thousands of bags of candy still come from Rose Confections.

Through the years, Brother de Paul has had many other Jewish friends. Among them, Joe Greenstein, a Minneapolis alderman, who helped get the House of Charity location on the northside approved by the City Council; Leonard Daniels, a member of the House of Charity Board of Directors; Rabbi Jay Goldberg from Temple Israel and Charlie Cohen, who lived at the House of Charity. Charlie, in his 80's, was a self-educated street philosopher. He had been a men's hat maker and had always paid his own way. He lived on his Social Security pension and considered the House of Charity his home. On Christmas Eve, 1979, Charlie died quietly. He was 86.

Chapter 28

In January, 1962, Brother de Paul persuaded the leaders from the missions that were still functioning, the Salvation Army, many Protestant ministers, the Jail Chaplains and Episcopalian Priests — about forty persons in all — to meet at the Normandy Hotel for dinner to celebrate the 10th anniversary of the founding of the House of Charity. It was the first time

that many of them had come so close to someone of a different faith. Even his community was very hesitant about going, and it took hours of persuading to have them attend. Dr. Spano was the only Board member who came. When they all realized in their prayer before the meal that they all invoked the same God, some of the barriers came down. Life long friendships developed from Brother de Paul's brave step into ecumenism. It was 28° below zero outside that evening, but very warm inside.

The next year Brother de Paul organized an ecumenical church tour. People of every faith who were interested in visiting Central Lutheran Church, St. Mary's Greek Orthodox Church, St. John's Lutheran Church, St. Mark's Episcopal Cathedral and Temple Israel Synagogue were taken by bus to these churches. A reporter and photographer from the Minneapolis Star and H. O. Sonnesyn from the Northside Post were on board for this historic "ice-breaking tour." At each house of worship the minister, rabbi or priest gave a tour and explained a little about their services. After the tour, they had an agape (love feast) at Cafe di Napoli to share fellowship. It was an historic, unforgettable day!!

At the eighth annual Charity Dinner, where the price was still $50 a couple, Brother de Paul reported that "last year we served 28,300 pounds of potatoes, 15,219 loaves of bread, 5,677 gallons of coffee, 3,014 pounds of onions, 51 bushels of apples, 78 crates of bananas, and 481 cases of lettuce. This is proof of the miracle of the loaves and fishes," he explained, "we didn't pay for any of it. I never liked paying for anything."

At this same dinner, Alice Codden, who was lovingly dubbed, "Brother Alice," was given the House of Charity's first Charity Award. Her tirelessness, her hours of unpaid overtime, her dauntless spirit of giving, her comraderie with the brothers, volunteers, workers and guests were remembered this night. Of her bookkeeping when she started working eight years ago, she confessed, "It was very simple to do the bank audit then — there wasn't any balance."

In March of 1963, three members of the Minneapolis Junior Chamber of Commerce came to see Brother de Paul. As they met in the small reception room, one of the men announced with a big smile, "We have a surprise for you."

"A surprise? For me? What is it?"

"You have been chosen to receive the Junior Chamber of Commerce Man of the Year Award for 1963. Isn't that great?"

Brother de Paul did not share their enthusiasm. He was the first candidate for such an award who said, "I want to think about it." He had to see if the award fit into his life as someone who is dedicated to serving the poor. It seemed to him that no one but politicians and successful businessmen had received the Distinguished Service Award before. The Jaycees were amazed that he didn't jump at the offer. "If you don't agree with a day's delay, then choose the next person in line. I must think about it and pray about it."

Brother de Paul felt that everything he did must fit into his philosophy or it was "no go." He did accept the award, and the publicity that went with it was fantastic; newspaper photos and stories, television appearances and a round of talks all over the state.

When Dr. Spano realized that Brother de Paul was getting his clothes from the clothing barrels, he insisted on buying him a new suit and shoes. He called the store and told the owner, "Don't let him take the cheapest suit and shoes. We want him to look nice for his many public appearances."

As the Minneapolis Man of the Year, Brother de Paul competed in the award for the 10 Outstanding Men of Minnesota, held in Albert Lea. Before he left with Dr. Spano, Alice and his sister, Lucille, a dear friend and generous benefactor called him. "I just wanted you to know that I hope you don't make it in Albert Lea!" Like a bolt out of the blue, it crushed Brother. As he was chosen one of the 10, he thought of his friend's wish, "I guess even those close to me might resent my getting this honor. It might diminish our relationship." This hurt.

For the past 10 years, since the first time Cedric Adams showed Brother de Paul's House of Charity on TV, Henry Wolf's and Phil Jones' appeals on their radio and television shows, George Grim's frequent mention in his column of Brother's accomplishments, to the hundreds of articles, both locally and nationally, and the many radio and television shows about the House of Charity, Brother de Paul felt this unsolicited coverage showed again the providence of God. He works in many, many ways.

Starting in October, 1963, when Brother de Paul dug the first shovelful of dirt during the ground breaking ceremonies for a new building on Nicollet Island, until the following summer, there was much construction activity. The old dining room buildings got sparkling, charming, white colonial fronts which pepped up what was left on the island. The dining rooms were so beautiful many people thought they were public restaurants.

Across the street, next to the residence, the new building was for the House of Bargains, with a full warehouse and repair shop in the basement. Selling second-hand furniture, clothes, jewelry, and housewares had become a good fund raiser and the volunteers, or Troubadors, needed more room to display their wares. By working long hours they were able to repay their loan in two years instead of five. When their store was all set up, they called it "Daytons on the Island," in deference to one of Minneapolis' leading department stores.

About this time the Salvation Army which had used a building on Nicollet Island, built a new $1 million social service center at 900 North Fourth St. At the Charity Dinner of 1964, Brother de Paul presented a plaque to Major John Troutt "in appreciation and admiration for your generosity and leadership in building a new social service center to better serve God and fellowmen."

Ed Brooks, one of the officers at the Salvation Army while it was still on the Island, and his wife, Birdie, became very good friends of Brother de Paul's. The first time Ed saw a line of men two blocks long on the bridge, he wondered where they were going. He followed them to the House of

Charity where he met Brother de Paul and heard about his work. According to Ed, "I always marvelled at the faith he had and the love he showed to the men and women he worked with and for."

Not everyone in Minneapolis shared this enthusiasm for the House of Charity and its work. At a meeting of the City Council Licenses Committee, the police license inspector told the committee that men coming to the House of Charity first line up on the bridge by the Great Northern depot "where they can be seen by our out-of-town visitors." Alderman Richard Kantorowitz added, "when these people get free food, that means they have money to buy liquor."

Another alderman, Robert McGregor, said "the free lunches are not necessary because anyone in need can be helped under existing government relief programs." The city relief system sometimes denied relief to problem drinkers in order to force them to seek care in Pioneer House, the city's alcoholic treatment center. "But this effort is defeated by the free meals at the House of Charity," the alderman complained.

There were numerous letters to the Editor supporting the House of Charity in its work with the poor. "What is so offensive in the sight of poverty? It is embarrassing, you feel uneasy, vaguely guilty and uncomfortable. But who said life was supposed to be comfortable?—This city can be proud to show its visitors that there is kindness and warmth for anybody, whoever he be; proud that there is a House of Charity."

And, "Please do not discontinue having free lunches on Nicollet Island. Many recipients are veterans of wars of our country."

Another wrote, "The Council should be thanking Brother de Paul rather than criticizing his contribution to society."

The House of Charity Board of Directors responded to the criticism with a resolution adopted at their meeting on December 6, 1964: "Whereas we are informed of derogatory remarks . . . it is the unanimous opinion that these statements are entirely unfounded and unjust . . .

"We consider these statements a great affront to the many thousands who devote their time, money and prayers toward the success of this organization. These include every denomination and walk of life." The resolution listed the organizations which had worked with the House of Charity and had acclaimed it. It mentioned other charitable work done by the House of Charity besides its food program. And it promised the continued operation to render assistance to "all persons of any race, color, sex or creed."

Brother de Paul, when asked in a television interview to respond to the criticism, said, "Sure, some people we serve take relief money and drink, but it's only a small percentage of those we feed. In any Christian program designed to raise standards of living, there are bound to be abuses." He pointed out that the House of Charity does not feed those who have been drinking heavily, and it operates its own alcoholic treatment program. "Many of those treated for alcoholism are met in the lunch-line."

One of the aldermen retracted his criticism in an article in the newspaper; the other one called Brother de Paul and apologized. When Alderman McGregor was chosen Man of the Year, Brother de Paul, the last year's recipient, made the presentation. The alderman suffered some tense moments as Brother de Paul introduced him, but all was friendship and forgiveness as the award was warmly presented and received.

Amidst the abuse Brother de Paul took periodically from critics of his program, there was usually someone or something to keep him from being discouraged. In the summers of the mid-sixties, the teenagers from the Catholic Youth Center provided this uplift. About 25 boys and girls came to the House of Charity to help cook and serve the meals. The staff and the people who came to eat were impressed with their youthful enthusiasm and dedication. These teenagers were called the Peace Corps J.G.

On Thanksgiving Day, 1964, the Brother de Paul Revue once again brought their annual song and dance fest to Stillwater State Prison. About 450 men were lifted into the holiday spirit when the house lights dimmed, the drums rolled, and a chorus line of young dancers, swinging lights, opened the show to the tune of "There's No Business Like Show Business."

Miss Minneapolis of 1963 made a big hit when she did a ballet-hula, wearing a grass skirt, and dancing to "Sentimental Journey."

Cyril Paul, a local singer who had performed at many House of Charity functions, and six young girls did a series of Calypso numbers including the "Amen Chorus." There were three very young girls who sang and danced and who probably had no idea of how many of the men in the audience were reminded of their own children. Gail Schreiber, a soprano, sang "Climb Every Mountain" and the words were meaningful to the men. Kay and Carol, operators of a School of Dance, were busy providing recorded music and getting the youngsters outfitted and on stage at the right times. Belinda Nissen sang some Joan Baez numbers and later joined Miss Minneapolis and Cyril Paul doing the Twist to rock and roll music.

The inmates gave the performers a standing ovation. The "Prison Mirror" expressed their feelings in its headline, "Stage Show is Smash Hit!"

Brother de Paul felt closer than ever to the prisoners since Roncalli House was opened. He had lived with murderers, stick-up men, "paper hangers" (bad check artists), child abandoners, and men who had committed assaults of all kinds — real tough characters. He had learned to give these men responsibility, but depending on them had to be guarded to prevent disasters in the operation. Mike, among many others, had taught him that. For the past several years, the House of Charity Mens' Club had supplied the food for the Brothers and about 30 residents to have a delicious Christmas dinner, after they had served over 400 people at the food center across the street. Mike, from Roncalli House, was to prepare the meal, but on Christmas Eve he was arrested. Brother de Paul went to the jail early on Christmas morning to see if he could get Mike released. The guard told him, "You'll have to call the judge." Brother de Paul took the chance of awakening him. "If he'll be back this evening, the guard can release him" the judge told Brother de Paul. Mike left the jail for the day and cooked a delicious Christmas dinner, but Brother de Paul sweat it out until he was back in jail that night.

A few days before the big line-up for Christmas, Phil Jones, a WCCO television reporter and later with CBS, showed the empty shelves at the House of Charity. The response was heartening. The Jewish Mayor of Minneapolis, Arthur Naftalin, sent over a 30-pound turkey with his chauffeur; James Ryan, on his way home from the Covered Wagon Restaurant, came to the door at two o'clock in the morning with a check for $200; Rev. Clarence Kilde from St. Mark's Episcopal Cathedral came over with money; 100 Christmas trees were donated to be given to poor families, and many envelopes arrived in the mail with a dollar bill or a check for five, ten or one-hundred dollars. Brother de Paul was convinced that God took care of the House of Charity's poor through these people. He also realized that Christmas Eve and Christmas Day were tough days for the men. Memories of happier ones tormented them and some of them found solace in drinking. Several times all the residents became intoxicated on Christmas Eve. For this reason the men had to check in by 4:00 p.m. on Christmas Eve or lose their residency. Brother felt this was for their own protection because the next day they would be filled with remorse and drink more than ever.

The chapel was always the central part of Christmas with poinsettias, lights, greens, and the Nativity scene. It was here that the brothers, the residents, and the workers were refueled and revitalized in their commitment to the poor, the lonely and the abandoned. They found strength in prayer at the feet of Jesus in the manger.

Chapter 29

Brother de Paul had always specified that the House of Charity fed and housed anyone who needed it, regardless of race. He had native Americans, Mexicans, Blacks and a few Jews besides the other people who ate, worked and lived with him.

When he saw what was happening to black people around the country in the mid-sixties, he was upset. As he watched the news on television one night, a sheriff was shown sicking a dog at some blacks. Brother de Paul jumped out of his chair saying, "I can't sit here comfortably while this goes on in the United States. I have to go down there."

He didn't have any money, but that didn't stop him. He told several friends that he'd like to go to Montgomery, Alabama to march with Martin Luther King and, voila, the necessary funds for travel came in. Mr. King was marching from Selma to Montgomery to end discrimination in voter registration. The Board of Directors didn't officially approve of his going. Dr. Spano, the President, said "I guess it's o.k. if you go as a private citizen." His family supported him 100% this time. On March 21, 1965 Brother de Paul flew to Alabama with his sleeping bag. He stayed outside of Montgomery in a complex called the City of St. Jude, where there was a church, a school and a hospital. It was raining when they arrived at the field where big tents had been set up for the crowd.

In the evening, in the Alabama mud, they had a camp gathering to bolster everyone's enthusiasm for the march the next day. Harry Belafonte, Pete Seeger, Sammy Davis, Jr., Billy Eckstine, the Chad Mitchell Trio and Tony Bennett put on a show for 15,000 persons. That night Brother de Paul left the camp to tour Montgomery even though he'd been warned of potential danger.

Fortified with bread and peanut butter the next morning they began a 12-hour march to the State Capitol in Montgomery. On the way they met Martin Luther King. As they walked through the black section, they were applauded. When they came to the white business area, they heard snide remarks. "You gonna shack up with one of those black gals tonight?" "Yankee, go home." The thousands of marchers sang "We Shall Overcome" as they walked along, at least one hundred times. On the highway a Minneapolis reporter spotted Brother de Paul and the next morning his name was on the front page of the Tribune.

Brother de Paul was impressed with the kindness and patience of everyone in the march. "With the lack of food, the rain and the mud and then the hot sun, there were no complaints. Each one believed in what he was doing, I guess."

On the plane back to Minneapolis, as he ate a full course dinner, Brother de Paul thought, "There's never been a meal that's tasted this good!"

The two brothers, Anthony who had come back to the House of Charity and Stephen, who were still "living in the community" found it harder and harder to live under Brother de Paul's constantly expanding mission. When he just had the food center and helped alcoholics, they felt they were following their chosen way of life, although it was tough and demanding. Now there were too many directions and too few workers — a residence for parolees, constant remodeling and moving around, the second-hand store and the new ecumenism. They opposed this, especially, because they felt it took too much time away from their community life. One of them told Brother de Paul, "You're giving up your faith, Brother."

He insisted "The House of Charity is ecumenical in support and purpose. We do not "push" the Roman Catholic faith, but I am personally loyal to its beliefs and traditions."

In frustration, discouragement and the knowledge that they could not commit themselves to this life long drudgery, one by one they had left. The brothers averaged about six years of service. On the way back from mass one noon, Alice Codden met Brother de Paul on the bridge. "Alice, the community is gone," he said despairingly, "how can we manage without them?" As they stood looking down at the Mississippi River, Alice assured him that he'd be able to carry on. She was a comfort in this time of despair. "I'll never leave," she promised. That night was a lonely one for Brother de Paul, one gripped with discouragement and despair. Prayer did not come easy.

The next morning, fortified with a desire to keep serving the poor, he did manage. He again took over the management of the dining room and re-assigned the various duties the community had done. It was a painful time of change, but also a time of growth. Graf Halverson, a volunteer and benefactor, gave Brother de Paul some consolation when he said, "These young men have done more to help people, no matter how short a time, than most of us do in our lifetime." It wasn't a waste.

Brother de Paul always respected and encouraged the faith of anyone he helped, but he wanted to make them more aware of God in their day to day living without preaching long sermons to them. This had been one of his purposes in founding the House of Charity. On October 6, 1965 the House of Charity had its first Ecumenical Scripture Service, with Father William Michel as the homilist. His theme was, "If you love God enough, your sins will lop off one by one." It was his last function as a clergyman. That night he had a heart attack and he died two weeks later.

The idea caught on even though some of the staff objected. Every Wednesday evening at 6:05 p.m. the men planned and participated in the communal worship. A different clergyman was invited each week to have dinner with the residents an hour before the service. Besides over 60 Catholic priests and 28 Lutheran ministers, homilists came from the Disciples of Christ, Presbyterian, Covenant, Church of God, Baptist, Orthodox, Episcopalian, Methodist, Assembly of God churches and the Salvation Army. These clergymen volunteered for a Wednesday evening service whenever Alice contacted them.

SPENDS HOURS IN PREPARATION for every talk . . . Father Anthony Coniaris, pastor of St. Mary's Greek Orthodox Church, spoke frequently in the interfaith chapel and his fantastic talks were pondered for a long time afterwards.

Choir groups and professional singers from the Twin Cities area sang at special services. Each week the residents chose the hymns that were most meaningful to them. A resident chose verses from scripture and he read them. Some of the men did very well; some were very nervous, especially if it was their first attempt at reading in public. It was a people-oriented service that developed close fellowship. Neighbors, benefactors, volunteers, and auxiliary members were invited and encouraged to come so that there would be "some of the outside" present.

Each participant could present any prayer intention that he wanted the community to pray for. They could bring all the events of the week to the Lord — sickness, problems in the house, birthdays, anniversaries, world events, accomplishments and blessings. The men who had experienced "ear banging" at the missions appreciated this open form of prayer. At the weekly meetings for house residents, John, from Alabama, suggested, "Let's make Wednesday dress-up night. It will make our worship service a little more special." It also gave them dignity and self-confidence as they were mistaken for board members by some of the outsiders who came to the services. Several of the "outsiders" who attended the Ecumenical Scripture Services asked to have their retirement/farewell services in the chapel. Rolf Stageberg, Superintendent of the Minneapolis Workhouse and Holger Jensen, Director of Minneapolis Relief, were among them. The Court Screening Committee met at a Wednesday evening service once a year and then went to a fellowship dinner to strengthen their ties.

Chapter
30

A few months before Christmas, 1965, Brother de Paul received a letter from Mark, a twenty-eight year old man, who was serving a ten-year sentence for grand larceny in an Alabama prison. He had heard about Roncalli House and he wondered if they could take him in when he was paroled.

"Brother de Paul, I have no one, nor any place to go. I have been an orphan since age five, and since that time I have been incarcerated in one institution or another. First, the orphanage, then to a Boys' School, then to a State Industrial School, where I started running away. I was then transferred to the State Reform School, and finally to prison here.

"Sir, I'm sure you would be able to give me the guidance and help I need to make a new life for myself. You are the only hope I have of ever getting out. Will you help me? Please?"

There were many letters from Mark, but when Brother de Paul sent him a fruitcake before Christmas, his letter of thanks was read to the residents assembled in the chapel for the Christmas Eve service:

"I can't begin to tell you of the happiness that is in my heart here tonight. When I received the package from you, I just couldn't believe it was really for me, until I seen it was from you. I've never gotten anything from anyone before, at Christmas or any other time. Believe me, I'll always be grateful to you for your kindness and your love for your fellow men, but especially toward me. This is the only time since I can remember that Christmas was ever anything to me except just another day, thanks to you!

"Brother de Paul, I realize I am a man full grown but tonite my heart is that of a young boy again. Is this so strange? You know I can't even remember being young. I have always felt that I was born an old man. If it never comes again, tonight I feel the true happiness a child or young boy must feel this time of year. It's a feeling I'll never forget."

A few years later, a member of the Good Samaritan League paid Brother de Paul's way to see Mark in prison. It was an ugly, depressing place, but when he and Mark met, the rapport was immediate. They talked for three hours. The day after Brother de Paul got back to Minneapolis, there was a letter in the mail.

"I cannot begin to tell you just how much your visiting me today meant," Mark wrote. "It was the happiest moment of my entire life. Just to know that after all those wasted years, I finally have found a sincere friend."

Chapter 31

As the Christmas season started, Brother de Paul really missed the stability and the hands of the former community. For the past thirteen years he had depended upon these men to supervise and work in the kitchen, dining room, office, the pick-up truck, laundry and in cleaning. Now, more than ever, he had to count on the residents and volunteers.

As he explained, "I knew I had to keep busy, keep going, keep it organized because we didn't want anything to be less than in previous years — just because there was no longer a community here.

"Alice Codden did more than anyone could expect of her; the volunteers and some of the men of the house came through with a fantastic Christmas dinner. I went to the jails, and the workhouses, had our worship service — kept busy all day."

When the day was over, Brother de Paul went into the quiet, beautifully decorated chapel where the spotlight shown on the Infant Jesus. Here he prayed on his knees for everyone he knew and loved, everyone who loved him, everyone who didn't love him. His thoughts and prayers included all his benefactors, his volunteers, his family and all the men who had ever come to the House of Charity. He thanked God for all these people, starting with his mother and father and encircling the world, and for allowing him to serve His poor. Brother de Paul felt so at peace after his chapel visit that it has become his traditional holy hour on Christmas night.

Another tradition was started after this first Christmas without the community. Charles Carey, who was on the Board of Directors and, in his 70's, became a priest, invited the staff, the volunteers, the live-in residents, Brother de Paul's family and special people on the Island to the "Embassy Room" of the Sheraton Ritz Hotel. It was called "Brother de Paul's

Christmas Family Night Party" because they were one big family. His mother was a special guest, enabling all the "family" to meet her. For some it was their only family. Each person, dressed in his/her best sat down to a steak dinner with many courses. There was singing by professional entertainers and throughout the evening each of the forty guests told what the House of Charity meant to him/her. Some of this brought tears, some, laughter. Ernie Johnson, one of the residents, in awe of the luxurious setting, said, "I wonder what the poor people are doing tonight!"

After several hours of comraderie, they got into a bus and toured the prize winning outdoor Christmas decorations. Some of the residents had never seen the brightly lighted homes in the city. The sounds of "Joy to the World," "Silent Night," and "Jingle Bells" drifted from the bus as they all sang, some off key. Everyone had such a good time, they didn't want the evening to end. "Family Night" was held every year the day after Christmas. Sometimes Brother de Paul's parents and family joined them, sometimes they went out for a birthday, and sometimes even for a "No occasion family night." It helped bind them together.

The volunteers had always been an integral part of the House of Charity, but now they were needed more than ever. Another second-hand store was opened at 2100 West Broadway which needed more helping hands. Every person Brother de Paul met was a potential helper. He'd wonder, "Has this person a contact, a talent, or some material help for our work?" He developed a volunteer system where men could come to live at the House of Charity for six months, a year, three years, or even five years. They were given their room and board, a small amount of money and a special area of responsibility. Some of these men were alcoholics, some stayed on from Roncalli House, some answered an ad in magazines, and some just came in "off the road." Each one was given some responsibility in the operation of the House of Charity and some discipline, with an 11:00 p.m. curfew and no drinking allowed on the premises. Brother de Paul tried to establish a "community" feeling — with mutual respect for each person, a feeling that had been lacking in many of their lives. The residence was to be kept homey, attractive, very clean and comfortable and the residents were solely responsible for this. They also took care of the House of Bargains warehouse, re-stocking the stores, making all the pick-ups with the two trucks, running the free dining room, helping in the office, helping with remodeling, repairing, and housekeeping, and assisting with Christmas projects and big mailings. They were also responsible for breakfast in the residence seven days a week. Sometimes when the person responsible did not show up, breakfast was coffee and rolls.

The House of Charity also needed local volunteers who would come in regularly and give of their time and talent. They were needed for office work, pricing and sorting for the second-hand stores, working at rummage sales, shoe repair, painting, religious counseling, printing, barbering, recreation room work, and A.A. counseling.

These volunteers had to have a full commitment to Brother de Paul's work. According to Alice Codden, "Brother is a perfectionist. You soon learn that only top level performance is acceptable and you find your self with the same high standards, or you forgot about it."

Some thought he went too far in his desire to keep everything at a very high level. All benefits were to have a theme, decorations and attractive invitations. "We're just having a dinner. Why all the fuss?" — or — "It's good enough for those poor people."

Brother tried to keep calm when he set them straight. "I don't feel that way. I won't allow anything to be second rate just because we're working with the poor." Some "forgot about it."

The Troubadors kept the House of Bargains stores open six days a week and two evenings. One 82-year old lady walked six bitter cold blocks from the bus stop every Monday evening to clerk in the store. By 1966, the Hennepin Avenue bridge had been condemned so buses stopped coming to the island.

There were many, many volunteers — Grace Fanning and Marie Fagerstrom who decorated the display windows in the House of Bargains; the college students who lived at the House of Charity throughout the school year and assumed a daily duty; a mother of eight children who solicited meat for the dining room; a father of nine who was in charge of the Saturday night game committee and brought his children along; ministers, priests, and seminarians who officiated at the Wednesday evening scripture service and thereby became involved with the men, and all the members of the Sunshine Club, the Good Samaritan League and the North Suburban Auxiliary. The Good Samaritan League had been primarily a Catholic auxiliary, and Brother de Paul wanted an inter-faith one to include Protestant women from the northern suburbs of Minneapolis. Thus the North Suburban Auxiliary was organized. The first 25 members were Lutheran, Catholic, Presbyterian and Methodist. These women made items to sell at the annual bazaar and also helped assemble the Christmas packages to be sent to Midwest institutions. Later, the Good Samaritan League had women of other faiths. Lillian Halvorsen, a Lutheran, became the first officer who was not Catholic.

Brother de Paul wrote in the North Minneapolis Post about his volunteers. "Those who work for the House of Charity will find a stronger purpose in their lives, they will feel more useful, and they will have the satisfaction that only those who serve their fellow human beings can have."

Chapter 32

The 15th anniversary of the founding of the House of Charity was cause for celebration. On April 27th there was a concelebrated mass of thanksgiving at Our Lady of Lourdes Church with eleven priests on the altar, the Protestant ministers and their wives in the front pews, and all the friends, and benefactors of the House of Charity joining in the prayers of Thanksgiving. As Brother de Paul had been decorating the church for the anniversary, Father Tom O'Donnell, the pastor, had told Alice, "When Brother is around I just step back and let him go, he's too fast for me!"

The Gospel according to Matthew was appropriate. "You are the salt of the earth. If it becomes insipid, how shall you restore its tang? Then it is good for nothing but to be trampled under foot. You are the light of the world. Men do not light a lamp and then put it under a bushel basket. They set it on a stand where it gives light to all in the house. In the same way your light must shine before men so that they may see your good deeds and glorify your heavenly Father."

The Rt. Rev. Monsignor John McEneaney from Brookings, South Dakota recounted in his homily the work that had been done in the last 15 years. He also tried to prick the conscience of anyone not involved. "Dedicated men here at the House of Charity have greeted their fellows as brethren in Christ — not only in word, but in deed and in truth. Out of the past, there stands with us tonight Francis of Assisi and Vincent de Paul who were witnesses in their times of the charity of Christ. And they rejoice that their example has drawn others to witness to that same love in this age. St. Matthew's gospel speaks of salt and light. At the House of Charity men have put the salt of love into the bit of bread that their brothers were eating and helped them to savor the joy and peace of God who is love. Here at the House of Charity men have lit a lamp that has given light to many who have walked in lonely darkness. . . . In the richest country in the world it is easy for us to neglect the poor of Christ. These are the very ones Jesus has identified himself with: the hungry, the homeless, the naked, the sick, the alcoholic, the drug addict, those in prison . . . the frightened, the lonely people who crave human affection. The people most of us can't stand and we don't want around.

"We have rushed to the suburbs to manicure our lawns and ignore our brothers in the slums. We have spent millions on super highways so that we can commute swiftly and comfortably and not see the areas where men have lost hope and are decaying. Most of us have so many opportunities to learn, to work, and to play that we can forget those who, burdened with human weakness, are caught in the swamp of poverty, alcohol, narcotics, and crime. The contrast is so great that we are easily repelled by the squalor of the slums, and we fail to perceive the inviolable dignity of our brothers who have fallen under the weight of their burdens.

"Thanks be to God tonight. To the God who touched the heart of Brother de Paul and his associates 15 years ago. God, who writes straight with crooked lines, sent him with 25¢ and His love to help His poor. . . . The work of the House of Charity was begun quietly, the money came as Brother de Paul knew it would. From an unbelief, nourished by despair, bitterness and frustration, many of the poor came to discover the honest concern of another human being who gave them bread and love.

"The work of the House of Charity has prospered because the power of love is irresistable. Sensitive people have given money, a dedicated few have given themselves, and many of those who were served have discovered what makes a man a real success.

"The work of the House of Charity is the living of the scriptures. The living of the scriptures tells us that Christ himself is to be served in the homeless, the naked, the sick, the imprisoned. We must lay down our lives for our brothers, and this word of the gospel is not an easy word to live by. Brother de Paul and his fellow brothers have lived by this word. They have gone into the alleys, the rooming houses, and the prisons to embrace — with that delicate sensitivity which only true love possesses. . . . By faith, we must also accept the mystery of His presence in these people, for he has said, "for what we do for one of these, the least of His brethren, we do for Him. Lord, strengthen our faith."

Chapter 33

The 15th anniversary celebration was a much needed shot in the arm for the House of Charity in its long struggle to exist. For the past two years the Housing and Redevelopment Authority had pegged the buildings along East Hennepin on Nicollet Island as the next target for the wrecker's ball. The businessmen, the Minneapolis Revival Mission, the Salvation Army, the House of Charity and everyone who owned property there united to fight this plan — and they won. Temporarily, they could stay on the island.

Then the East Hennepin Avenue bridge was declared unsafe and closed for repairs, and a decision was made to build a twin bridge to carry one-way traffic. The island people couldn't win on this one — they would have to move.

It was a heartbreaking thought because Brother de Paul and all his workers loved being on the island. Each one of them had worked so hard to build the various dining rooms, the chapel, the dormitories, the residence across the street, and the House of Bargains. Now it all would be toppled. They felt they were surrounded by water and by community and they didn't think they'd find another place like it. Gloom and despair gripped many of the residents, the volunteers and the people they served. Brother de Paul asked for their prayers at this critical time in finding a new home.

Every Christmas since Brother de Paul and Brother Martin first shared their makeshift chapel in 1952, Christmas Eve has been a memorable time. The candlelight ceremony, the singing of the carols, and the reading of the story of Christ's birth has always brought the feeling of togetherness, of warmth and of love to the people of the House of Charity.

Brother de Paul had another dream, though. He wanted to have a Catholic mass celebrated in the chapel on Christmas Eve. Most of the residents at the House of Charity were excited about having a mass on Christmas Eve — some of them were Catholic, some had been Catholic, but they all were welcome. Dick Thorpe, one of the men who worked in the warehouse, was chosen to be an altar boy and he was thrilled about it. Dick had come to the House of Charity for alcoholism treatment — to start a new life. Two days before Christmas, as Dick was driving with Brother de Paul, Brother asked, "Dick, how long has it been since you received the sacraments?"

"Oh, boy, maybe 15 or 17 years."

"I've been praying for you, Dick. Why don't you go to confession, then to Communion and straighten out yourself spiritually?"

"Well, I don't want to face the priest before he says our mass. Confession after all these years will be damn tough."

"You can take the car and go to some neighboring church."

Dick looked at Brother de Paul and saw his concern. The next day Dick wanted the keys to the car. When he came back two hours later, he was beaming with happiness. Brother de Paul noticed the change and asked, "What happened, Dick?"

"Well, Brother, I went to the church, but I just couldn't get out of the car. I drove around, and I drove around, and finally, I said to myself, "Get some guts, Dick. I went to confession and cleansed my soul for the first time in years. The priest was great to me."

Before the mass, with all those who shared his pioneer days crammed into the little chapel, Brother de Paul conducted the candlelight ceremony which all the House of Charity "family" loved. When he turned off all the lights, Florence Beck, the organist, couldn't see her music. One of the School Sisters of Notre Dame nuns who had come to sing, lit a candle for her and put it on top of the organ. As Florence, who volunteered for 20 years, played the Christmas hymns, the candle wobbled and fell, spilling wax on the nun's habit.

Before Father Al Janicke began the mass, he looked at Brother de Paul's radiant face. "We've waited a long time for this celebration — to bring the Body and Blood of Christ on the altar to the House of Love." Joe Ligocki, the 80-year old man who repaired furniture in the House of Bargains, read the epistle in his raspy, choked up voice, and Dick Thorpe was the altar "boy."

As Brother de Paul watched Dick on the altar, serving mass with meticulous response and devotion, he couldn't help think of Dick's family — somewhere, hurting. At least Dick had restored his relationship with God.

When Dick left the House of Charity the next September, Brother de Paul never heard from him. About three years later, as he was greeting the men in the line-up on East Hennepin Avenue, a fellow asked, "Are you Brother de Paul?"

"Yes, I am."

"Well, I've come to tell you about Dick Thorpe. He talked about you a lot. We were both working on a banana boat near Mobile, Alabama. A few weeks ago, when he was sitting on the railing of the boat, he slipped and fell into the water. He couldn't swim. He drowned. I felt I had to come and tell you about Dick."

Brother de Paul was saddened by the news of Dick Thorpe's death, but he thanked God that Dick could have had the happiness, the renewal, and the restoration that Christmas Eve at midnight mass.

Chapter 34

East Hennepin Avenue on Nicollet Island had continued to function as a remnant of Skid Row through most of the 1960's, but the Barber Shop, the Island Liquor Store, the bars and the Island Cycle Supply Company gradually gave up and moved or quit. The Minneapolis Housing and Redevelopment Authority told Brother de Paul that the south side building, the dining room, could be used for a few more years, but the newly built House of Bargains and the newly remodeled residence on the north side of the street had to be abandoned by the next year — 1969.

Where could they go? What would it cost? Who could help them re-locate? Brother de Paul felt that the city of Minneapolis, as long as they were forcing the House of Charity to move, was obligated to see that it was properly resettled. He wrote to the Mayor and to some of the city aldermen but he didn't get any response. Months went by and Brother de Paul was getting panicky. He wrote to clergymen and benefactors throughout the city to explain how he felt there were political moves to "strangle" the House of Charity out of existence.

With support from these friends and many others and with his own acceptance of the challenge, he was ready to continue his service to others, wherever the Lord would lead him.

By summer of 1968, the House of Charity was close to finding a new home. The Unity Settlement House at 250 17th Av. North which the Good Samaritan League rented for their monthly card parties, was for sale, privately.

First, a hearing was held by the Minneapolis Planning Commission to determine whether the House of Charity program would be acceptable in the area. They delayed their decision after residents in the area expressed concern over how the new establishment might affect the community. A long time supportor, Father P.W. Coates, pastor of nearby Ascension Church, and Alderman Joe Greenstein helped the northsiders understand the purpose of the House of Charity. This alleviated their fears. The Minneapolis City Council would not give the necessary legal permits until the House of Charity went to the people of North Minneapolis and had open hearings. The Jewish section, the Black section and the Catholic section each had a chance to ask some harsh questions of Brother de Paul and to vote on whether or not to accept the House of Charity. Almost 100% voted in favor. They bought Unity House for $75,000. For the first time in 17

THIRD HOUSE OF CHARITY at 250-17th Avenue North.

years Brother de Paul would have his own office. For the first time they would have grass and trees. The new home was large and stately, with white pillars on the front, but it needed much remodeling to have the bedrooms, kitchen, dining area, meeting rooms and chapel fit the needs of the House of Charity and pass inspection by the city. As usual, Brother de Paul presented the project to "his men." "This is your home, boys. Let's see what you can do with it." The men responded to this challenge; they put in long days, sometimes it was difficult to get them to quit working. They liked to be given a sense of dignity and responsibility.

In November, 1968, while everyone at the House of Charity was helping with preparations for the move to the North side, vandals broke into their building around the corner from Unity House. It was to be used as an administrative area. They broke every window pane, destroyed furniture, tore doors off the walls, smashed bathroom fixtures and started a fire in the basement. Damage estimate was $35,000. The building had to be completely destroyed. Brother de Paul said, "I don't know of anyone who would have such strong feelings against us to cause so much damage." The news media made a big story out of this and Brother and his staff feared the main building might be vandalized, too. Lights were put on all sides and a security guard was hired for a month to watch the building at night.

The Christmas of 1968 was unusually hectic because of the planned move to the northside. Amidst the frustrations and joys of it all, American Express offered Brother de Paul a week in Mexico if he would be a tour guide. He could get away from the problems, relax and be with people.

While in Mexico, the founder volunteered to fight a bull, not full grown, but still, a bull. Wearing the full regalia of a matador, with a few basic instructions, he took the colorful cape and with shouts of "Ole! Ole!" from his tour group, he entered the ring. In a short time, the bull knocked Brother de Paul to the ground and he had to be rescued. For his challenge he received a certificate and an injured foot.

When Carol Pine of the North Hennepin Post wrote a national prize winning feature story about the House of Charity in the January 23, 1969 issue, she told the history of its programs and how it operated. When she asked Brother de Paul how the House of Charity survived with no guaranteed financial support, he answered, "We are always betting that there are ample people who are really concerned enough to contribute. With all our tremendous plans we never know where the money is coming from next."

These "tremendous plans" included building a "massive charity complex" that would house all the House of Charity services plus a proposed senior citizens' tower with living quarters, temporary accommodations for persons and families on relief, and an interfaith chapel at the center of the complex.

1969 was a busy year for the House of Charity. There was the usual Charity Dinner in February, the St. Patrick's Day Dinner in March, all the annual traditions of Lent, Holy Week and Easter Sunday, plus the work going on at the new location in North Minneapolis.

At the end of April, Alice Codden sent out a letter announcing Brother de Paul's 40th birthday on April 28th. She enclosed an article from the Minneapolis Tribune telling about the work he had done for the last 17 years. "How was such a huge undertaking started and carried on:

with NO Government Grants
with NO Church underwriting his projects and
with NO United Fund assistance?

"How? By begging — begging — begging. Whether it be for food for his daily line-up on the bridge, volunteers to run his salvage stores, or money to pay the countless bills of the two Halfway Houses, he was and is asking for others. What better time than his birthday to give him our prayers and our support in his building program?"

Brother de Paul needed these prayers and support because it bothered him to turn 40. He had accepted graying hair at age 35, but now he felt "middle-aged." Yet during the week of his birthday he joined hundreds of others and walked 18 miles in rain and a late season snow to raise money for hungry people in the annual "WALK FOR MANKIND."

On April 30th there was a special birthday Scripture Service, where Rev. Leo Vetvick, the Court Chaplain who came to the Ecumenical Service frequently gave the homily. He told how he felt a kindred spirit with Brother de Paul. They both dedicated to the oppressed, the lonely, the down-trodden and the alcoholic who could be all of these. He praised Brother de Paul for recognizing human dignity in these people.

The Holy Name Catholic Church Choir under the capable direction of Warner Wagner, a part of so many House of Charity celebrations, sang several hymns and were joined by the whole congregation when they sang the "Happy Birthday" song.

A few months later, Rev. Leo Vetvick and Brother de Paul and others began the Court Screening Committee for Alcoholics, a voluntary group representing organizations involved in work with alcoholics. They made recommendations to the judges of what was best for the man or woman. This was the beginning for getting alcoholics out of the drunk court and into treatment. Rev. Vetvick led the way in eliminating the inhuman, degrading "drunk tank." When they began their daily trek to the courthouse, which put a "hole" in Brother's schedule, there were as many as 125 bleary-eyed "drunks" on Monday and about half that many through the week. They would be sent to the workhouse for two weeks to "dry out" and then to the Old Pioneer House, a Union City Mission center that kept them off the streets.

In 1971 the state legislature passed a law that prohibited arresting anyone who was drunk. Instead, they were placed in a detoxification center and were counseled and given the option of going for treatment to the Salvation Army, the House of Charity, the New Pioneer House or another treatment center. The whole concept of alcoholism began to change.

In between his two birthday celebrations, on Saturday, April 26th, Brother de Paul was busy selling at the House of Bargains. From 9:30 in the morning until 5 o'clock in the evening, he parted with over 100 Madonna statues that he had been given from all over the world. It had taken him twenty years to collect them; less than eight hours to sell them. The total sales were over $1,000.00, and all of this money was earmarked for the starving people of Biafra. These people had been fighting for independence from Nigeria for over two years, and their food supply had been cut off. This was the beginning of Brother de Paul's work with starving people all over the world.

Chapter 35

Brother de Paul wrote his friends, "You are invited to the recitation of the rosary at 3:15 p.m. on Sunday, June 1, 1969 at the second floor chapel on the Island.

"We would love to have you with us as we pray the rosary for the last time before we move the altar, the Crucifix, the drapes and the pews to our new location in North Minneapolis." The next day, the move began. One of the symbols of the House of Charity, the statue of Christ lighted in the window was left on the island for more than a year. After the House of Charity received the money for the property, the statue was crated very carefully for the ride to the Northside. So many men had come to love Christ through seeing His work done at the House of Charity. The statue had been in the window on Nicollet Island almost from the beginning and with the sun shining on it, the paint had peeled. The statue of Christ was repainted in its new home.

After the last Wednesday evening Ecumenical Service in the chapel on the Island, with Father William J. Ward as the homilist, the congregation took the bible, the hymnals, the candles, etc., and walked more than two miles to the new House of Charity. As they marched up Washington Avenue, they sang hymns and they concluded their service in the chapel on the northside. Refreshments also awaited them in their new home.

On Sunday, June 29th, the residents, Brother's family, friends, the volunteers, the benefactors, the Board of Directors, priests and ministers gathered for the dedication of the Ecumenical Chapel of Jesus, Our Brother. This name was chosen by Brother de Paul to show the kinship all these people had with the Lord.

At 2:00 p.m. the House of Charity A.A. Group had their first meeting in the new location. At 5:30 p.m. after a short tour of the new facility, guests enjoyed Beverly Culligan's concert on the new organ that was donated by the Good Samaritan League. For the dedication ceremony, Brother de Paul called on many of his friends who had been a part of the House of Charity. Joyce Meyer, who had participated in the Thanksgiving Day shows for many years, sang "Let There Be Peace on Earth," "Bless This House", "You'll never Walk Alone" and Etta Bye accompanied her. Alice Codden, the dedicated House of Charity office manager, read the list of deceased residents. Harold Busk, the warehouse foreman, read from Scripture and then Rev. J. Millard Ahlstrom, a long-time Lutheran friend, led the prayer. Brother de Paul's Salvation Army friends, from Nicollet Island days, Ed and Birdie Brooks came from Ft. Dodge, Iowa, for the ceremony and they sang, "What A Friend We Have in Jesus" and "Without Him." The hot, humid temperatures in the high nineties did not damper the enthusiasm of anyone during the long ecumenical service of dedication of this chapel. Carl Fox, who considered himself Brother de Paul's "gospel singer" sang "Panis Angelicus" and "Ave Maria" accompanied by Beverly Culligan. The Rev. Clarence Kilde of St. Mark's Episcopal Cathedral led a prayer of thanksgiving and petition. Monsignor P.W. Coates, pastor of Ascension Church nearby, and a loyal friend for many years who helped make this location possible, blessed the chapel. The residents, in their own words, asked God's blessing on the chapel as they stood around the altar. Brother de Paul told about the successful move that had been accomplished with everyone's help. Father James Donovan, a Paulist Father from St. Lawrence Church, who counseled the A.A. men each Thursday, gave the prayer of Thanksgiving. With everyone holding hands to show their love, their strength and true fellowship, the congregation prayed the Lord's Prayer. To conclude the dedication ceremony, everyone sang the hymn that was sung every week at the Ecumenical Service — "How Great Thou Art." —

O Lord My God! When I in awesome wonder
Consider all the worlds Thy hands have made,
I see the stars, I hear the rolling thunder,
Thy pow'r throughout the universe displayed.

REFRAIN: Then sings my soul, my Saviour God to Thee
           How great thou art, how great thou art
           Then sings my soul, my Saviour God to Thee
           How Great thou art, how great thou art.

When through the woods and forest glades I wander
And hear the birds sing sweetly in the trees

When I look down from lofty mountain grandeur
And hear the brook and feel the gentle breeze.

And when I think that God, His son not sparing
Sent him to die, I scarce can take it in,
That on the cross, my burden gladly bearing
He bled and died to take away my sin.

When Christ shall come with shout of acclamation
And take me home, what joy shall fill my heart,
Then I shall bow in humble adoration
And there proclaim, my God, how great thou art.

While all these people who were dear to him sang enthusiastically, Brother de Paul was moved to go from one to another and greet each with a hug or handshake. He felt such warmth that he has done this at every ecumenical service since.

When Dick Spurck had been "dry" for eight months, he read an ad in a national newspaper. "Volunteer needed. If you would like to give some time to the House of Charity, poor pay, long hours, write us."

"That's what I need right now," Dick thought to himself. "This first year of sobriety is tough, and there aren't many support groups out here in Montana."

He answered the ad and moved to the House of Charity. Dick did some driving and some counseling with other alcoholics. He had been drinking from the time he was sixteen until he quit at age thirty-five, so he knew what each man was going through. He was also in charge when the founder went to conferences, overnight visits to prisons or on retreats.

When Dick worked in the dining room he announced over the loud speaker that "there's a vacancy in the rehab program. If any of you men are interested in staying sober, see me after you eat."

One of the men Dick dragged off the streets was Don Lebak. Don had been drinking since World War II, had never married, and was in the line-up at the House of Charity dining room when Dick explained A.A. to him. Don had been a printer for a Minneapolis paper, but had drunk his way out of a job. He joined A.A., moved into Talbot House, and before long he was managing the dining room. Don got along well with his 10-man crew. Most of them were alcoholics like himself, so he knew their troubles and spoke their language.

Dick Spurck worked at the House of Charity off and on for two years, then he went to Iowa for training and is now working in the Probation office in Cedar Rapids, Iowa.

Another man, Frank Roberts, from New York, answered one of the ads, too. He flew to Minneapolis to see what the "poor pay, long hours, free room and board and $15.00 a week" was all about. He liked what he saw and stayed for over five years.

Frank drove the food truck six days a week, picking up food from regular donors, plus finding new ones. Hours meant nothing to him. He chauffeured senior citizens around, had picnics for them, drove them home every Wednesday evening after chapel services and worked in the dining room on holidays. Everyone loved this tall, thin, understanding young man with the ready smile. Frank was only 18 years old when he came to the House of Charity; at 23 he returned to New York, tired but happy he had been able to devote five years of his life to helping the poor. Martin Arens from Chicago volunteered as bookkeeper for one year. Generous volunteers helped to save a lot of money!

Remodeling to comply with housing, fire and health regulations and moving the House of Charity to the Northside was expensive, even with all the volunteer help. The City of Minneapolis bought the property on Nicollet Island for $230,897.65 but had not paid for it yet. When Brother de Paul was desperate for money to pay the bills even for everyday operations, he received a surprise gift.

A few days before the chapel dedication, Monsignor Rudolph Bandas, from St. Agnes Church in St. Paul, died. Brother de Paul had met him many years ago when he served Christmas Mass for him at Holy Cross Church.

After Monsignor Bandas was buried, his secretary called the House of Charity. "Brother de Paul, I'd like to have you come over to St. Agnes'. I have something for you."

A week later, when Brother de Paul met her, she handed him an envelope. "Here's a bond for $3800. It doesn't have to be probated or go through court. He bought it for you and your work when he was alive and well. Monsignor admired you for your work with the poor."

"Once again, God's providence," Brother thought as he rode the bus back to Minneapolis. When Archbishop Leo Byrne heard of the House of Charity's financial bind, he sent a personal check for $5,000. According to Brother de Paul, Archbishop Byrne "was always kind, fatherly and understanding. He was a genuine shepherd."

After 17 years on Nicollet Island it was hard for Brother de Paul to leave. In his column in the North Minneapolis Post he wrote: "My heart is still on the island and no doubt it will take years to change my feelings. When the highrises and commercial buildings replace the old buildings presently there, then I will just have the memories.

"I know everyone on Nicollet Island and they were all a part of the House of Charity. It's difficult to explain how I feel about the island — only experiences coupled with love can give one such an attachment to this slum area.

"The new neighbors here on the Northside are beginning to have familiar faces. My prayer is that within a short time they will have good feelings toward us and we can consider them part of our family."

The dining room was still on Nicollet Island and the men took the van or bus over six days a week to prepare and serve free meals to anyone who was hungry and poor. Don Lebak continued to manage the dining room with his ever-changing staff. Some of the men who came for treatment for their alcoholism stayed for a month, some stayed several months, a year, or even three years. It all depended upon how much of his life pattern had to be changed. While these men lived at the House of Charity they either worked in one of the projects such as the feeding program or House of Bargains or they paid board and room. Two hundred sixteen men went through the A.A. oriented program in 1969.

Chapter 36

A few days before Christmas, the first one for the House of Charity in the Northside, Brother de Paul invited all the kids in the neighborhood to come to his house. They sat around a manger scene and talked about what Christmas meant to each of them. To some it was the birth of Christ; to others it was a new pair of skates. They laughed and joked as they ate the fruit and candy Brother de Paul had for each boy and girl. "I don't have any kids of my own," he said with a slight tinge of regret, "but I love them dearly."

The residents at the House of Charity took invitations to their new neighbors on the Northside. They invited them to stop in on Christmas Eve to share in the mass and candlelight service or to come to the Open House on Christmas Day. About 80 people came and were surprised to see the happy, caring, neatly dressed and combed men who had moved to their neighborhood.

For the last 17 Christmases, Brother de Paul had been too busy to spend time with his family, and this bothered him. He decided to combine Christmas Eve with his community and with his family. His father, mother, brothers, sisters, nieces and nephews, about 26 in all, came early to share this time with him in the meeting room. While they ate and exchanged gifts, Brother de Paul visited with them, popped in and out, ate a little with them, took care of last minute details, then came back and visited some more. The Kondrak family participated in the traditional candlelight ceremony and then stayed for the Christmas Eve mass. Everyone in the family enjoyed this time, even shared time, so much it became an annual get-together.

It was the 18th Christmas at the House of Charity. Earlier in the year, at the Charity Dinner, a county sheriff had told Brother de Paul, "Anything I can ever do for you, just let me know."

Brother de Paul had called him a few days later, "I know it's a little early," he said, "but I would like your permission to bring some carolers to the jail on Christmas Day."

"Gee, Brother, we usually don't let anyone in on a holiday like that. There's a shortage of guards, you know."

Brother de Paul convinced the sheriff that caroling would add a bit of Christmas cheer to the prisoners' bleak day. Many months later, he carried out his plan, and he wrote about it in several newspapers.

"CHRISTMAS MORNING! What a beautiful, tremendous feeling, almost of exultation! It runs from the littlest child to the oldest senior citizen, but you and I know there are many, many exceptions. For how many will this be a day to bear up, caught in their own webs of loneliness, with only past Christmases and memories to keep them from despair?

"Among many such places, a jail is bleak on Christmas morning. The bars separate humans from each other. Not a decoration, not a tree, not a sprig of holly or evergreen can be found. Because of visits in past years here on the morning of this festive day, I had made arrangements in advance with the proper authorities to allow myself and about 10 Benedictine Sisters into the jail proper to sing carols.

"The Sisters had rehearsed for weeks in anticipation of this new experience of bringing Christ's love to the imprisoned on His birthday! The weather was below zero that Christmas morn; we all had trouble starting cars, and so we arrived late.

"The Sisters were a little nervous, apparently because not one had ever been in a jail even on a visit. We took the elevator up and the conversations and jokes were the usual ones when we try to cover our apprehensions.

"We encountered the guard on duty — a big, burly fellow. He startled all of us by saying that he was not going to let us in. I promptly informed him that we had authorization and that he could verify it with a phone call. He frightened the Sisters by telling them the men might be very rude, curse them, embarrass them, etc.

"I then huddled with the Sisters in the hallway. I told them they would have to decide whether to press the issue

to get in and do our planned caroling. They talked it over and then said something like, 'we certainly can't be frightened off by this or where is our commitment to Him?' We talked and argued until we were let in, warned again that the 'Sisters might be sorry.'"

"We headed for the solitary block and were impressed with the warm smiles and response we received. I have never heard such fine caroling. The 'Carol of the Bells' made a big hit because the Sisters were carrying little bells to match the melody. We went slowly through the jail, even arousing some from sleep. Their eyes expressed their appreciation. Some lay in bed listening and right beside them was the Christmas gift bag from the House of Charity.

"We went into the women's section and sang a cheery song for them, too. What impressed the nuns was a young man who was picked up late Christmas Eve for heavy drinking and put in jail for his own protection. The Sisters went directly into his cell and sang the "Carol of the Drums." He looked like a boy to us.

"The Sisters wanted to sing a carol for the attendant who had resisted us so much at our entrance, but he shocked these good women by saying, 'I had enough of that last night' (apparently meaning church services or carols). We thanked him anyway and started to leave the building.

"The Sisters were thrilled but they wanted me (they were all teachers) to grade their performance. I could see they were pleased. 'Sisters, you all get an A plus,' I said, 'because you were a howling success.' Not one moment of anything improper was heard from the men.

"As I wished them holiday greetings and said goodbye, heading toward the Island Dining Room to feed our many guests, I knew that we had not changed the lives of the inmates. But we had preached a great sermon, because we had let them know that as Christians, we cared.

"Isn't that what Christmas is all about?"

The Troubadors, the volunteers who ran the House of Bargains, had built up a good business in their new building on the island, and had donated thousands of dollars to the House of Charity. When the north side of East Hennepin Avenue was to be demolished, they had to move. The #2 House of Bargains had been opened at 2100 West Broadway several years ago and it did so well, the Troubadors moved their #1 store to 1007 West Broadway.

One of the volunteers, Mrs. Walter Therres, had worked in the island store and on West Broadway. She found the new location very different. "Down there it was mostly transients, here it's mostly familes."

About 50 volunteers ran both stores, putting in 8778 hours in 1970. Brother de Paul felt the House of Bargains was an outlet for these people to do something useful for their community. They provided low-priced clothing and household needs for families with limited income and they raised money for the House of Charity. In 1970 their sales totaled $34,061.87.

Nine months after the House of Charity was barely moved and settled at 250 17th Avenue North, Brother de Paul got a letter from the Minnesota Highway Department. The new freeway to be built through north Minneapolis would run right through their property. Once again, they would have to move. Brother de Paul trembled as he read the letter to everyone in the chapel that Wednesday evening. The service was like a funeral. "Dear God, what do we do now?" Brother prayed.

He had had such big plans for the House of Charity on the North side. His "Charity Complex" to serve the poor, the senior citizens, the alcoholic had been his dream and now it would be squelched with the wrecker's ball. Tragic, burdensome, and busy yes, but always exciting!!

Brother de Paul asked for prayers from everyone at the service that they would find another place to locate the House of Charity. The search began in the spring of 1970.

Chapter 37

On Sunday, April 28, 1929, the day Brother de Paul was born, one of the front page stories in the Minneapolis newspaper told that "Paul Chapman, head of United States Lines, announced the company would inaugurate a trans-Atlantic air liner service. Passengers to Europe will have a choice of going by steamship or airplane. If they are in a hurry, we'll put them across in 24 hours or so in an airliner."

Forty-one years later, as a birthday present from his many friends, Brother de Paul took a "trans-Atlantic air liner" to Moscow — in nine hours. For over 20 years he had been praying for the conversion of Russia, and now he had the opportunity to visit this center of communism. The American Express tour arrived on the weekend of May Day, which is a holiday. Red flags and huge photos of Lenin were everywhere. Their guide, Irene, spoke perfect English, was very affable and smiled a lot. She told Brother de Paul she had never been to church in her entire life. Brother de Paul knew that the Russian state had replaced God and religion, but he was overwhelmed with the complete secular movement leaving out everything spiritual. He prayed, "Oh, God, no one here knows you and still you love them."

Brother de Paul found that Russian women were equal to men; they fueled airplanes, drove and unloaded trucks, swept streets, as well as taught school and practiced medicine. He felt the fear that the Russian people had about talking to the Americans. As he walked around Red Square late at night, praying the rosary for peace, he noted how different this was from Fatima. "God, do you hear prayers from this atheistic country?" He met an Orthodox Monk, Father Ambrosi, and attended a 2½ hour evening mass at his monastery. The other monks resented his presence at the supper table.

He also went to mass at the only Catholic churches in Moscow and Leningrad. The friendly pastor in Leningrad gave Brother a piece of rock from his church as a souvenir, as that was all he had to give. Brother felt deeply that both were his brothers.

After spending a week in Russia, Brother de Paul felt rather distressed. No one trusted another person. The totalitarian government, controlled by communists, owned and operated every business, every theater, every utility. With changed flights, long delays and many complications in getting his Polish visa, Brother learned a word used very often in Russia — nyet (no).

When Brother de Paul arrived in Warsaw, Poland, his aunt Lucja and cousins Izabella, Stephania and Marta came to the Hotel Europejski to meet him. The warmth of their meeting, with an exchange of gifts and flowers, was a welcome relief from the restrictive silence and coolness in Russia. With Brother's limited, broken Polish, Marta's little knowledge of English, and a Polish- English dictionary, they enjoyed two days of visiting, walking around Warsaw, attending an opera and watching a colorful parade that celebrated the 25th anniversary of V-E Day. This was the first time any of the Kondraks in the United States had met their relatives in Poland since Brother de Paul's father had left there 56 years ago. They worshipped together in Holy Cross Church, the name of his home church in Minneapolis.

The Catholic churches were open and filled for worship, people talked without fear, the damaged buildings of World War II had been reconstructed, mini-skirts were prevalent and the whole atmosphere of Warsaw seemed Western to Brother.

When the American Express tour group arrived in Bucharest, Romania, it was hot and humid. No American publications were allowed, so they had had very little news from the United States. Brother de Paul was grateful for the transistor radio his sister Lucille had given him; he could listen to the "Voice of America." In a letter home he wrote "Without the 'Voice of America' the cause of freedom and religion would be lost behind the Iron Curtain. We Christians everywhere must become very zealous, or we will be lost. We must never take our Christianity for granted. We must, as His followers, speak out against any injustice. The vestment of a famous bishop in Russia had 15,000 pearls sewed on it. The Emperor's horses had silver horseshoes nailed with silver nails — while peasants lived almost as animals. Christianity should have been more effective in helping them to a better life.''

From Bucharest the tour continued to Budapest, Hungary where from Brother de Paul's hotel room, he looked down at the beautiful Danube River. In this city of antiquity, he saw once beautiful churches run down, in need of repair and almost abandoned. It was in Budapest that Cardinal

Mindszenty was living in exile at the American Embassy and Brother de Paul walked to a small park next to the Embassy to pray for him. In his letter home, Brother wrote: "Just think, for years Cardinal Mindszenty has been living in the American Embassy and has never been allowed out. A policeman stands on duty 24 hours a day. How we take our religion for granted! . . . Always remember that it is the treasured gift of free speech that makes America great."

When the group arrived in Vienna by sailing up the Danube River, everyone felt the freer atmosphere. They had spent three weeks behind the Iron Curtain and they had felt the restrictions imposed by the communist rule. The founder was thrilled to attend mass on Pentecost Sunday at St. Stephen's Cathedral where he enjoyed the world famous Vienna Boy's Choir, a real treat.

From Vienna they went to East and West Berlin by bus, through the beautiful "Sound of Music" country. The infamous Wall between the free and the Russian controlled parts of Berlin gave Brother de Paul a quick and sad comparison between freedom and captivity. He was thrilled to move on to the familiar shrines of Lourdes and Fatima to pray about his trip behind the horrid "Iron Curtain," and then to Minneapolis.

In his last letter home, he wrote: "Materially, much from America and the Western countries is influencing these countries behind the Iron Curtain in dress, music, transportation, etc. But I am very sorry to report that spiritually we are giving very little, if anything at all, to these people."

At the tour's farewell party, the people guessed that Brother de Paul was either a Wall Street broker or a C.I.A. Agent. He had left the group so often by himself.

Chapter 38

On August 5, 1970, one of the few remaining apartment buildings on East Hennepin Avenue burned, taking the lives of 11 aged victims, all known by Brother de Paul. One of them was to become a full-time resident that very day. Three of them, Dewey Petrie, Joe Ryan and Joseph Milligoss had frequently been in the food line at the House of Charity. They had no known relatives.

On the following Saturday morning, Brother de Paul arranged for an outdoor ecumenical funeral service for the three men on the front porch of the House of Charity under the majestic white pillars. With about 150 friends, 18 of them acting as pallbearers, they had the ringing of the bells, and the singing of the Battle Hymn of the Republic. Prayers and scriptures were led by Rev. Leo Vetvick, the court chaplain, Father Dan Finnane, a summer volunteer from Wisconsin, and Rev. Bill Russell, Church of the Nazarene, Chaplain at the Minneapolis Workhouse, and special hymns were sung by Joyce Meyer with Florence Beck, the regular volunteer organist playing an organ given for the purpose of the funeral. All artists who came to any service contributed their service gratis and willingly, so they could share in the noble work of the needy at the House of Charity.

The Founder followed with his personal feelings about these men whom he knew well and the need for decent housing for every person. As they prayed the Lord's Prayer, the mourners held hands around each of the three caskets to show their unity, love, and kinship with the three men. Three little girls placed a red rose on each coffin. The founder's words were heard that night on television news when the funeral and burial were shown to the public. The "little people" were very, very important to Brother de Paul and he wanted them to have a decent burial, worthy of the dignity of someone created by GOD. GOD cared about them and so did the House of Charity "family."

With the sale of the property on Nicollet Island, the purchase of Unity House, and then the further search for a new location, the House of Charity's founder and the board of directors had many decisions to make. Brother de Paul felt the pressure and anxiety more than the individual board members, because the work for the poor was his whole life.

In his monthly reports to the board of directors in September and October, 1970, he showed his deep sadness and bitter disappointment in their poor response to House of Charity gatherings. "A member of the board of directors has been working with the owners of the property that we are interested in on Marshall Avenue Northeast. He will report at the next meeting. The Housing and Redevelopment Authority has offered us $47,691 for the two buildings which compose the Island dining room. There were no board members present for the social hour to kick off my $2,000 Special Needs Fund. . . . Our building fund is $37,050.93." The founder had worked "day and night" to beg for this money so that there would be funds to begin construction at the new site.

On the 18th of November the board of directors met about the purchase of the land on Marshall Avenue Northeast, and they passed this resolution: "Contingent upon discussing the sale of this property located at Marshall St. N.E. with the owner, the board of directors hereby authorizes the acquisition of the property." The motion carried by a 6 to 1 vote. The founder voted "No" only in respect to the purchase price of $210,000.00. In arranging the final agreement he wanted the motion to specify $10,000 less as it would make the negotiating easier if the resolution limited the amount to $200,000.00. He always wanted to get everything at the lowest price possible and did not want to pay more than was absolutely necessary. He did get the agreement to read "$200,000.00." It was one of many "scraps" with the board over matters he considered very important as he raised the funds. One member in defense said that they insisted on the bigger amount because they did not want to call a special meeting just in case it was not acceptable. But the founder felt one more meeting to save $10,000 was acceptable to him as a workable procedure for such big money.

"LOVE SERVES THE POOR" had been the motto of the apostolate ever since a national magazine article about the work had entitled the story in the same way. This motto was on the postage machine so that every piece of mail that went out would remind the recipient of the ever important purpose of the organization serving the poor.

But for the founder the "poor" included many other people, not just those on skid row. The annual Thanksgiving show at Stillwater State Prison brought the Jaakaola Dancers, the Gene Thomas Orchestra and the Jolly Brothers, accordionist Jerry Zelanzy, drummer Mike Wendolek and "Big

Mama," Dorothy Freyberger. Over the years there was a long list of talented people who got up early to arrive on time at the prison. The shows had to start early enough so the prisoners could be fed afterwards and be locked up as on holidays the security crew was small in the afternoons. In fact it took "a lot of fast talking" by Brother de Paul to convince the wardens to allow the troupe in on the actual holiday.

The 785 prisoners and guests were ecstatic as the Jaakkola Dancers set the pace for the two-hour "De Paul Revue" with a lively rendition of "Dark Eyes." The Jolly Brothers played favorite polka and popular numbers like "Rain Drops" and "Mrs. Robinson." "Big Mama," or "Everybody's Mother," Dorothy Freyberger, shook the rafters with her singing "Harper Valley PTA," "Bill Bailey" and "Tiny Bubbles." She earned one of the most generous ovations ever extended to an entertainer at the prison.

Two weeks later, in the Prison Mirror newspaper under her picture was "A Special Thanks to Dorothy."

"The Prison Mirror recently learned of the tragic death of little Janette Freyberger, who was killed in a car-horse accident on November 11th, one month ago.

"The feature story of this issue reports on the Thanksgiving Day show which was staged and produced largely because of the good will and generosity of Janette's mother, Dorothy Freyberger. She thrilled the prison audience with many special numbers.

"In her time of grief she proved that she could give of her love to others less fortunate, in spite of her great loss."

In answer to Brother de Paul's 1970 Christmas appeal letter to 26,652 persons, 2465 responded with $25,507.21. When he sent out a reminder to those who had not contributed at Christmas time, in January, the total jumped to $41,174.06.

This was the third year of Brother's personal crusade to enlist people to look for someone who needs their love on the actual holiday. He felt many wonderful things were done for lonely people before Christmas, but too many benevolent givers wanted Christmas Day for themselves. The founder had strong deep seated convictions about sharing with and serving needy people on the actual holidays.

His list published in the North Minneapolis Post was endless: "senior citizens, residents in nursing homes, inmates in jails, workhouses and prisons, widowed persons down the street, patients in hospitals and mental institutions, foreign students, men in the armed forces, people sitting in hotel lobbies, or a single person sitting at a table in a restaurant.

"We all have possibilities," he concluded, "let us look to see if we have locked up Christmas in ourselves. The answer will be this Christmas Day if the newborn Christ finds anyone within our reach who is still lonely, cold, unfed and forgotten. A check to your favorite charity helps, but never fulfills our personal responsibility to share.''

Two letters, written to him on Christmas Eve, reinforced Brother de Paul's apostolate of love. One man from the Hennepin County Jail, told of his feelings. ''Christmas has a special meaning for all, but maybe a little more for us in here because we are away from our families. . . . Your kindness brought our sad hearts, low morale and dying love a little more hope in mankind. . . . Maybe, maybe God didn't forget me after all.''

The second man, from the Minneapolis Workhouse, wrote thanking Brother de Paul for caring and then, ''Your enclosed prayer has given me peace of mind and helped overcome some of the loneliness I feel on this night.''

The down payment of $50,000 was made for the purchase of the three acres of land at 2000 Marshall St. Northeast and Brother de Paul's dreams were about to be fulfilled. The House of Charity complex would include a rehabilitation center for 60 persons and six staff members, a 300 seat chapel overlooking the Mississippi River and a residence tower for 70 senior citizens.

He began working with a generous and talented architect, George McGuire, to design the three buildings in a very futuristic squared design. The landscape would be beautifully terraced to the river. To achieve this development, though, the zoning laws would have to be changed.

On March 15, 1971, a hearing before the City Planning Commission committee attracted a crowd of 350 people from Northeast Minneapolis. For one hour and 20 minutes a few of this citizens' group told how they thought Brother de Paul was doing good work, but ''don't bring it to our neighborhood.'' Most were more antagonistic. They called the men ''bums, drunks, and sex perverts.'' One man feared for his children being ''accosted by this type of derelict.'' ''Don't bring the 'garbage' here.''

A woman got up and announced, ''We want Brother de Paul to know that we feel God helps those who help themselves. We're sick and tired of helping these people. Let them get out on their own.''

Brother de Paul was surprised and hurt by this small but well-organized resistance group which opposed the House of Charity's building plans. He told them that in 19 years there had not been any violence, not even a serious scuffle inside the building.

When the City Planning Commission Committee recommended denial of a zoning change, Brother de Paul responded, ''I'm just disappointed in the Christian response I saw here today. I'm a Northeast boy myself and I'm ashamed.''

Calls and letters from friends and benefactors of the House of Charity came to the Mayor of Minneapolis, Charles Stenvig, to Minneapolis aldermen and to Brother de Paul.

Father Stan Sledz, the associate pastor at Holy Cross Church in Northeast Minneapolis, inserted his views and feelings in the Parish bulletin:

"Since I've been here at Holy Cross, I've been inside the House of Charity (now located over North) several times to celebrate Mass, preach at Scripture Services, and eat with these 'ex-cons,' 'drunks,' 'perverts,' and 'bums' (names they are called). This already puts me in a greater advantage than any of the people quoted by the people in the Star. The advantage is that I dared to go there, meet some of them, and eat with them. Now I am not afraid of them. I was taught to be afraid of them in the same way as we are 'taught' to be afraid of policemen, our boss, rich or powerful people, Negroes, Indians, teachers, priests, nuns, and tax collectors. People scare us. People who don't know themselves, who are scared themselves.

"I'll be glad to go with you to the House of Charity sometime (250-17th Avenue North). I purposely put this address so that you realize that we are not talking about the 'soup line' on the Island. We are talking about a residence building for reformed alcoholics and men released from jail who are adjusting to society. It's a 'half-way house.' The entire house is immaculately clean (and remember, we're talking about male residents only). The atmosphere is happy, yet shy. That's very different from the image we get from movies, isn't it? It's also as close to St. Philips and Ascension Schools as this new location would be to ours, yet no child has ever been attacked in the two years they have lived there.

"This is the only kind of building he will put up, besides a chapel and a home for the aged. Knowing this, and other facts which I have shared with you from my experience, I feel that many of us have over-reacted terribly and in a very un-Christian way. There can be no doubt in our mind that what Brother de Paul is doing is exactly what Jesus is asking each one of us to do. We have to take that 'date' also. If I could be objective with myself, I'd have to admit that I was insincere if I said, 'I admire Brother de Paul's work but I don't want it near me.' If that were my attitude and I lived at the time Jesus walked on earth, I wouldn't want him to move in my neighborhood either, would I?

"It isn't easy or glamorous to love the poor. Occasionally, we'll get hurt by what they say or do, as we

would by any person, rich or poor. But, ultimately, our treatment of the poor will determine whether or not we experience heaven. Jesus said that!"

—*Father Stan*

Much of Father Stan's message was included in Robert T. Smith's column in the Minneapolis Tribune, March 23, 1971. The issue was going to the City Zoning and Planning Committee this day and Robert Smith hoped this commission would be more sympathetic than the vocal dissenters.

But it wasn't. The Planning Commission turned down the request for a change of zoning upon recommendation of their hearing committee which had listened to all the northeast residents' protests. Brother de Paul could have brought his request to the Minneapolis City Council, but instead, he withdrew his application. Alderman Al Hofstede from N.E. shouted in a burst of anger to the founder, "We've heard about enough from you. I've gotten enough annoying phone calls from your supporters." Later as mayor of Minneapolis he would write a warm letter of recommendation about Brother de Paul to the Mayor of Dacca.

"Forgive and forget," commented Brother as he happily carried the mayor's letter on his next trip to Bangladesh.

"We won't move there if the neighbors don't want us," he told the Planning Commission, trying to hide his painful disappointment. That evening he made the same statement on television news. Brother felt devastated; he had been turned down by his "own" people. Some of the nuns who had come to the House of Charity many times told his sister, Lucille, that they were afraid to come now for fear of threatened violence they had heard about first hand.

People wrote more letters supporting Brother de Paul, and some came from northeast Minneapolis. Many had money enclosed. There were letters to the editor, both for and against the House of Charity. In a front page story of the Brooklyn Center and Brooklyn Park Sun Newspaper, volunteers Leslie and Flora Rogge, who had helped the founder for many years, testified that they had always been treated with respect by the men. One editor asked, "Where are the offers from other neighborhoods for the House of Charity to make their home with them?" The Northeast Ministerial Association met with Brother at lunch to encourage him, but they felt they could do little to change the protesters' minds and hearts. The controversy was in the news daily.

It had been a sad and disheartening experience and Brother de Paul felt "his" men had been attacked unmercifully. He thought the House of Charity would be an asset to any neighborhood. The following night at the weekly scripture service, these men, who had been found unwelcome in Northeast Minneapolis, prayed for God's help to find a new location. With tears in their eyes, they prayed for Brother de Paul and his work and asked God's blessing on those who had opposed them. There seemed to be no bitterness or hatred in these men's hearts, just quiet resignation. They had been put down one more time.

Two weeks later, on Good Friday morning, Brother de Paul held a service of reconciliation in the big empty lot at 2000 Marshall St. N.E., the site of all the controversy. Just before he left home, he had a call threatening his life, but he hid his anxiety from the group. One of the residents held a cross made from two rough beams as Brother led a prayer asking forgiveness for the anger, the bitterness and the resentment that had been shown by the people involved. It was a prayer service of love. The owner of the land returned the down payment. He was not required to do so.

The effects of this controversy apparently didn't drift down to the children in the area. One of the happiest days in Brother's life was when they proclaimed Brother de Paul Day at Holy Cross Grade School where he had graduated some 28 years before. Two 8th grade students had interviewed him on tape asking him questions about his work with the poor. Then the youngsters invited him to speak to the entire school.

When Brother de Paul arrived at Holy Cross School, he saw hundreds of signs, each in a child's own words and design, welcoming him. "Welcome to *our* Brother de Paul," "Welcome to your school." One made by a first grade girl had a tall, gangly man with a sign "we love you brothur de paul."

The two 8th grade students who had interviewed Brother were in charge of the program. They introduced him and presented him with canned goods for the poor. When he walked on stage amid their applause, he was almost speechless. Usually, Brother found it easy to talk to a crowd, but this time it was difficult. These were the children of some of the people who wouldn't let him build his House of Charity in Northeast Minneapolis. He thanked them for the honor and recognition they had given to "one of their own." He tried to create in them a deeper love for people of every race, creed or economic level.

When Brother de Paul went home he was thrilled with what he had witnessed. There was great hope for the future generation of Northeast Minneapolis — his old home.

After the Minneapolis Housing and Redevelopment Authority paid for all the House of Charity's property on Nicollet Island, they began to rent the dining room facility to them for $119 per month. This was a temporary, month-to-month arrangement because the buildings would be torn down in the next year. Now Brother de Paul was looking for two new locations and with the recent strong feelings of opposition it was humanly almost "unbearable."

But it was Easter, a special time of hope. He invited the poor and lonely men and women to come to the last Easter dinner to be served on the island. There was a colored egg for each guest, decorated and contributed by the Good Samaritan League. After 19 years of struggling to feed the hungry from the small table that fed 5 or 6 on the second floor to the beautiful panelled dining room they used now, Brother de Paul felt a part of himself would be going with the wrecker's ball. He loved Nicollet Island.

Chapter 39

The financial picture of the House of Charity had changed when they received the $230,000 for their island property, $10,000 from the Charity dinner, over $41,000 from the Christmas Appeal letter, and they now had about $60,000 in their building fund.

The board of directors felt that now the House of Charity should be run like a big business. The approach of the board officially about so many issues seemed to be at variance with those of the founder.

Personality differences caused some of the problems. "But," Brother de Paul said, "jealousy crept in, too. I recall informing all of the board about winning 'the highest award for the prize winning envelope' from the Envelope Institute of America, a national award in the summer of 1971. I received no comment in any form from the board members. It was discouraging because an artist of Hub Daly, who has a printing firm, worked so hard on our logo and our envelope. It got to me."

The Board proposed a study be made of the Halfway and Alcoholic programs at the House of Charity and they also requested that Brother de Paul furnish them with a breakdown of where the residents in these two programs came from and their present status.

Brother de Paul had always made decisions and had had the approval of the Board of Directors. This new approach of questioning his methods hurt. He was the founder, the executive director, the treasurer, the fund raiser, besides having been the cook, the laundryman, the cleaning man, the "beggar," the counselor and the man in charge of running the House of Charity.

When some of his employees heard that the board was questioning his management, they wrote a letter telling them of their loyalty to Brother de Paul.

"To Whom It May Concern: The House of Charity, 250 17th Ave. No., Minneapolis, MN., stands as a tribute and memorial to the capable and trustworthy administration of its founder, our employer and friend, Brother de Paul.

"We who are employed here at the House share his burdens and joys and are keenly aware of the care and consideration he gives to every detail.

"His demand for order and cleanliness, his sound financial judgement and his concern for mankind make Brother de Paul 'one in a million.'

"His program consists of work and discipline — helping each man to help himself and others.

"Nineteen years of operation steadily increasing in outreach and resources — beginning with hopes, dreams and a twenty-five cent piece and standing proudly today a Christian service that has served countless thousands — this we believe speaks out loud and clear in behalf of its founder and director, Brother de Paul.

"We have been informed that Brother's methods and policies of performing the Christian works of mercy are presently under criticism, and we who work for him are proud to say we trust his administrative judgement and give him our undivided and full support in carrying out the purposes for which he started the House of Charity."

It was signed by the warehouse foreman, the dining room foreman, the switchboard operator, the cook, the bookkeeper, the housekeeper and Brother de Paul's faithful secretary.

On July 9 Brother de Paul wrote to the board members, "Am in the midst of preparing a complete explanation of all the aspects of the House of Charity in its service to people.

"We are very proud of what has been accomplished in the last 19 years in our unique operation. . . .

"As I review the House of Charity, I now realize how much experimentation, how much growth and how much trial and error we have endured to come to our present stage. It was not easy.

"The main point to keep in mind is that our entire work is built on trust in the Providence of God and is not a typical social welfare agency. It must be judged from this standpoint.

"Secondly, one must be familiar with the founding and the entire history before one truly appreciates the present status and present mode of operation. Only in its proper historical context can it be properly and truly understood.

"Please remember those two very important points when reading my report.

"I ask for your patience; I will send you the copy as soon as it is ready."

In the first report, an eight-page story of the development of the free dining room, Brother de Paul told the purpose he had in mind when he started to feed the hungry men who came to the island. In opposition to the missions, which required attendance at their services before being fed, the House of Charity fed people because they were hungry. They have never had to turn anyone down because there was no food. He described the meals that were served and the crew who served them. The residents who lived on the North side were responsible for cooking, serving and cleaning up and Brother de Paul commended them for doing a very good job.

William Salzer, an employee of St. Edward's Catholic Church, was paid by the church to stay at the House of Charity for two weeks and to survey their work. The results of his survey were included in the report. He found that during the two-week period, of the 463 different men and women served, 332 were white, 102 Indians and 29 blacks. The ages ranged from 11 to 90, but the most were between 40 and 60. The length of stay in Minneapolis varied from one day to 80 years; 110 had been in the city from one day to six months, 383 of them lived alone.

The founder said, "I made it a daily practice whenever humanly possible to be at the dining room during the feeding time. I try to learn as many names of the people as I can. I truly feel the dining room is the heart of the House of Charity and the heart of the city."

Brother de Paul told of the many groups, mostly young adults, who have toured the dining room. "They eat a meal with the other guests to get the 'feel' of the place and also to discourage putting the poor people on display. A good percentage are Protestant high school students from the city and rural areas. The Lutheran Encounter Group visits each year and their response in thank you letters has been very encouraging."

The report went on to say that from the very beginning the House of Charity has had a Food Handling and Restaurant license from the city and state. We have complied with their every request and have an excellent rating each year after inspection.

"There have been thousands and thousands of persons who have come to know Christ through our love and concern for them expressed in our dining room during a trying time in their lives.

"In conclusion, the House of Charity Dining Room, founded 19 years ago, is to present to the poor and hungry and isolated ones, Christ's love for them through us in the form of the corporal works of mercy. It is as necessary today in our big cities as it was in the days of Christ as He fed the multitudes on the hills of Palestine."

The second report to the Board of Directors described the Emergency Services performed by the House of Charity. At the dining room, a person who can't come at meal time can get a sandwich, fruit, sweet roll and beverage. At the Northside residence, families can get a food order by filling out a short form and bringing the $15 certificate to a Red Owl store. They can get free surplus food at the Island Dining Room, too.

Clothing certificates for a specified amount can be taken to one of the second hand stores and the recipients can choose what they need.

If furniture is available at one of the stores, a certificate for a specified amount is given and they can choose the items.

Families in need of housing at night after the agencies are closed, are given a letter which entitles them to stay at the Andrews Hotel for the night.

Families are also referred to other agencies for long term care.

Individual requests for food are handled the same as for families. Clothing is given directly from warehouse supplies. For housing, letters are given to men for the YMCA and to women for the YWCA.

The hundreds of requests for assistance and information come from individuals, priests, ministers, rabbis, police, firemen, hospitals, public officials, custodians at jails, workhouses and prisons, hotels, A.A. Clubs, parole officers, judges, lawyers and doctors. They ask about separated spouses, suicides, funerals, reasonable hotel location, who to turn themselves in to at the police department, travel information, nursing homes to recommend and many, many want to know how to locate their lost loved ones.

The third and last report submitted by Brother de Paul to the Board of Directors told of his philosophy in working with God's poor and rejected. These are his guidelines:

— Create "COMMUNITY" in the house — staff, residents and volunteers all living and working together with mutual respect for each person and the community — this presents our biggest challenge and yet our greatest success because of the many isolated, "loner-type" individuals admitted. Journalists have written that we "touch the lives of people" here — and this is our main goal as a live-in residence.

— Give true dignity to these men who have lost so much of their self-worth before GOD and their neighbors. Helping them by our examples and attitudes to accept that they are children of GOD and to act accordingly to share our common lives at the house as brothers.

— Challenge them with all of the responsibility they can handle as individuals and as teams in various departments of our operation. Couple this with kind discipline and order, so lacking in their lives and thinking.

— Make exposure obligatory, realizing that acceptance must be an individual and voluntary action. We can present a setting, but the real desire must come from within the individual.

— Restore to society only when realistic that the resident can function on his own. For chronic "skidrow" alcoholics, one must exercise great care so as not to create another failure. With ex-offenders, depending on the length of prison experience and offense, a shorter time in residence is necessary.

— Face the discouraging fact honestly and squarely that there are some men who may have to be institutionalized, either periodically or for life, because of their severe handicaps. We would be unfair to this individual if this were not faced realistically. Nineteen years in this apostolate has proved this. It does not mean our efforts cease to restore him to society, but time proves valuable when twinned with much trial, error, and Christian patience. Long terms of residency are needed for many.

— Realize each day more fully that GOD is the center of our home and work here — and that most changes take place in a man through His grace, very often through A.A. and prayer. Although Catholicism is never promoted we strive very earnestly to restore a man to his former religious beliefs.

— Strive that we be not a duplicate of any other house, program, or institution and therefore keep our program unique for those whom we serve.

— Be constantly aware that we do not become a typical welfare or social agency but always mindful that we are spiritually oriented (not, however, denominational). We were founded for the unique approach, attitude, and service which has been carried out thus far in our history, to be truly a HOUSE OF CHARITY, a house of love.

— Make every effort always and consistently to keep our residence homey, attractive, very clean, comfortable, and to make the residents themselves responsible for this.

— Oppose vigorously any techniques which offend, experiment with, or "upset" the residents — or in any way degrade them psychologically, religiously or even mentally.

Also in this report, the founder explained the religious structure, the ecumenical scripture services, the counseling available, the daily rosary and the weekly mass. No one is compelled to attend any of these services, but the Christian atmosphere in the House of Charity draws many back to their faith. He told of his work with Alcoholics Anonymous, the Sunday meetings conducted by visiting squads, the Friday evening closed meetings by and for the residents, and that a van was available at least twice a week for outside meetings. The counselors are always recovering alcoholics. In working with "hard core" drinkers from skid row the basic concept has been upgrading rather than rehabilitation (in most cases this implies something they never had). After taking care of their basic needs, food, shelter and clothing, the second step is to keep them sober as long as possible. A man who has been drinking nonstop for 15 years has achieved a great deal when he is sober for 90 days. It gives him confidence to strive again for longer periods and slowly reverses his poor self-image.

Then using fictitious names, Brother de Paul gave a brief resume of 23 residents who were living at the House of Charity. Ranging in age from 27 to 76, seven were released from prison, 14 were alcoholics and two were looking for guidance to achieve some meaning or goal in their lives. Most of the men have no close family ties, most are looking for employment, some have had one or two years of sobriety and most of them enjoy living and working at the House of Charity.

Brother de Paul spent weeks getting this report ready for the Board and he thought it would cover the "study" they wanted done on the House of Charity.

He had suggested that no board meetings be held until his report was completed, but they met without him. A motion was made, seconded and carried that wage and fringe benefits of the staff and employees be obtained immediately.

The board discussed the matter of a salary for Brother de Paul. They felt he should have Social Security benefits like the other employees. At this stage in his life, the founder felt no need for a weekly salary. He resented the urging of one member that he be insured for a huge amount so there would be money to carry on the work after his death. It did not seem appropriate to him who felt very deeply that it was GOD, the provider, who had made everything possible for the House of Charity.

The final motion, seconded and carried, authorized and directed the President to appoint a three-man Executive Committee which would have the authority of the Board of Directors in the management of the business of the House of Charity in the interval between regular meetings. This committee would be subject to the control and direction of the Board with the exception that said Executive Committee shall not have the authority to expend or borrow in excess of $10,000 in any one transaction without prior approval of the Board.

Brother de Paul was upset, he was angry. When one board member insisted that one of the employees at the House of Charity receive severance pay after he was fired, Brother wrote to each board member. "Either the board member goes, or I go." The Board of Directors met and voted to withdraw money from the savings account to make the severance payment and to give the board member a vote of confidence. They also discussed three possible sites for the dining hall and decided to get more information before the next meeting.

One of the situations that bothered Brother de Paul was the way the members of the Board of Directors were chosen. He suggested an election by auxiliary and other groups so that the board would not be chosen by itself.

Twenty-seven members of the Good Samaritan League signed a letter to the Board of Directors: "We have just learned to our complete amazement and disappointment, at our monthly meeting, that you are criticizing Brother de Paul in his handling of the House of Charity.

"We have worked so closely with him for many years and thoroughly agree with the way we have seen him operate with his deep trust in God's providence.

"We want it known that we individually, and as the Good Samaritan League would volunteer *only* as long as Brother de Paul would want our help."

Chapter 40

In between the Fall Bazaar, the feeding program and the busy schedule for the residents, the arguments between the founder and the board continued. They couldn't agree on limiting the length of time a member could serve on the board. Few people realized Brother de Paul's problems with his health, his frequent surgeries, and how confrontations and stress effected his physical well being.

Many agreed that better communication and a broader representation on the board were necessary, but they didn't have concrete methods to achieve these goals. The board wanted to have an Independent Study made "without delay and hold itself in readiness to consider and act on its recommendations." They thought the study might recommend a way to make broader representation on the board.

Brother de Paul didn't agree that "a study would be so all inclusive as to even consider this aspect, which, I feel, is so urgent for greater understanding of me and my work at the House of Charity."

Because the date was changed, Brother was unable to attend the October board meeting but he asked that their differences be resolved. "Much time has been wasted during these past few months and I must have some satisfactory word from the board so we can begin to plan our Christmas here at the House of Charity. It means so much to thousands of persons."

Thanksgiving was here and the show must go on. Dorothy Freyberger, "Everybody's Mother," had promised Brother de Paul that she would entertain the prisoners with her rock and country songs at both St. Cloud and Stillwater. With a tight schedule and almost 100 miles between the towns, she wondered how she'd manage.

A Minneapolis businessman who was a benefactor of the House of Charity had the answer. He hired a helicopter from Imperial Airways that dropped Dorothy and Brother de Paul at Stillwater at 8:00 a.m. When she belted out "Bill Bailey Won't You Please Come Home?" as her opening number, the ovation from the prisoners touched her heart. Two hours later, they did a repeat performance in St. Cloud. Brother went on to the Dining Room to share the last Thanksgiving dinner on the island; Dorothy went home to prepare a holiday dinner for her family. When a lady in Stillwater watched the news on television and saw Brother getting out of the helicopter, she was so impressed with his work she left him $25,000 in her will, for his work.

The Christmas schedule of gift-giving, feeding and visiting went on even though the spirit of the past 19 years in the community was not up to capacity. Brother de Paul had sent a letter to each member of the Board of Directors asking for an improvement in their relationship:

"As we prepare to celebrate the beautiful season of CHRISTMAS, I am hoping and praying that there will be greater understanding between me and the board of directors.

"As I look back at the last part of the year, I can see that this has not been accomplished.

"I have submitted complete reports on our programs here and they speak for themselves; I would be willing to improve them.

"As I prepare for Christmas and the thousands we will extend our love to, I can only pray that this lack of understanding will not jeopardize the very existence of the HOUSE OF CHARITY.

"I can only say honestly that I intend to carry on the work I founded with GOD's help 20 years ago — no matter what form or under what "umbrella" it is as a non-profit corporation.

"May I ask for your prayers and then use this occasion to wish you and your loved ones a blessed holiday season filled with the joy and peace that only HE can give.

—Brother de Paul

P.S. At this stage, the response to the Christmas mail appeal is good but we may have to make a public appeal for food."

There was no response, verbally or in writing from the board.

Brother de Paul's family came to share Christmas Eve, the candlelight service where the nuns from the nearby Ascension Church convent sang carols and the Christmas Eve mass.

On Christmas Day the last Christmas dinner was served in the island dining room and many workers, friends and neighbors stopped in for the Open House at the Northside residence. At 6:00 p.m. the Rev. H. Dalton

Meyer from Calvary Memorial Church conducted the Christmas Night Service.

The New Year's Eve ecumenical service was always popular with the residents. Brother de Paul's long-time friend, Rev. Dr. Forrest Richeson, was the clergyman at the candlelight observance. Dr. Richeson had worked with A.A. since 1945 and had helped Brother back in 1953 when the House of Charity A.A. group was formed. Since that time he has been a popular speaker at their meetings, a counselor in the spiritual steps, and the annual speaker at the New Year's Eve service, even when he was very ill.

Chapter 41

The disagreements between the Board of Directors and the founder continued from time to time about different issues, but the day to day service of the poor and hungry never suffered. Brother de Paul insisted it be kept a simple performance of the works of mercy depending upon the providence of God. He felt that because most of the board members did not share the philosophy, the ideals and the goals of the House of Charity and its founder, they should all resign. After much prayer and inner pain, he requested their resignations. Two members, Jane Wolf and Leonard Daniels, both sympathetic to Brother de Paul, resigned; the others stayed on.

The Annual Charity Dinner was cancelled. In his letter to the Board of Directors Brother de Paul wrote: "I cannot be responsible for such a big undertaking which takes so much time, sacrifice and organizing when the attitude of the board indicates such a lack of understanding of our goals."

There were questions from friends and benefactors about the cancelled dinner. Brother decided to explain what was happening in his Easter letter:

"Because you have been so wonderful and generous to me in my work for GOD's poor and abandoned ones, I would like to share this problem with you confidentially.

"For several months now the present Board of Directors of the House of Charity has attempted to make changes which I am convinced are not within the concept of the work as I founded it 20 years ago. I have lived happily at the House of Charity all of these terrific years without a salary, wanting only to serve GOD and his poor ones. I have always attempted to improve and change as the challenge presented itself, but I will *not* stand by and let the House of Charity become another social welfare agency. I have always wanted the House of Charity to be a people place, not a program place.

"Am certain that you realize that the House of Charity is unique in its service to those persons who are not cared for by any other group. As founder, I regard very highly the works of mercy as commanded by Christ, and they are the foundation of my work.

"There are many fine organizations doing great work, but our uniqueness of *trusting* in GOD to provide our needs, of serving the desperately poor, and dedicating ourselves within this philosophy, is valued tremendously in the community as your fine support proves. Most outstanding has been our free Dining Room located on Nicollet Island which has served millions of hot, nourishing meals.

"The present board is a group of fine people; of this there is no doubt. But we must form a new board with greater cross section of experience and involvement in this type of work. (Our 3 hard working auxiliaries are not even represented on the board.) After long hours of discussion, many reports, etc., I felt that the only recourse I had was to ask the board to resign. Immediately upon my request, two board members resigned. I need a board who will work *with* me and guide me for our future needs, but all within the philosophy of our founding 20 years ago. I am on the board for life.

"Our other problem is still finding a new location.

"Please *pray* as these are serious problems.

"As usual on this Easter we will be serving many of GOD's poor in various ways — you share in this service of love.

"Thank you for all of your help — I felt that you who support our work must know its present crisis. A BLESSED EASTER to you and your loved ones is my prayer!!"

—Brother de Paul
FOUNDER-DIRECTOR

On Thursday, July 27, 1972 at 1 o'clock in the afternoon, two masked men with guns appeared at the Harry C. Piper, Jr. home in Orono, about 15 miles west of Minneapolis.

"Where's your old man?" one of them asked Virginia Piper, the wife of the president of a brokerage firm.

"He's not here," she began as they forced handcuffs on her and put a pillowcase over her head. They ordered her to lie down in the back seat of their car as they drove to Jay Cooke State Park, southwest of Duluth.

The kidnappers had left a note asking for $1,000,000 and the next evening they telephoned instructions for Harry Piper to pay the ransom. He borrowed the money, 50 thousand $20 bills, and followed their circuitous directions. At his request, the F.B.I. did not follow him, but the agents believed the ransom money was taken from the trunk of the car while Harry was in a bar at 424 Plymouth Avenue North carrying out the kidnappers' instructions.

About 1:00 p.m. the next day, Saturday, the F.B.I. agents were in the underbrush at Jay Cooke State Park where they followed a voice calling for help. About 48 hours after her abduction, Virginia Piper was found. The kidnappers, according to a news report, had telephoned "two clergymen" who had, in turn, called the police.

That Saturday morning, Alice Codden, the faithful secretary at the House of Charity, had been working the switchboard when a man's voice had demanded "I must talk to Brother de Paul!" Brother was on a retreat at the Trappist Monastery in Dubuque, Iowa.

"I'm sorry, he's not available. Can I help you in any way?"

The caller had explained he was calling about Virginia Piper and where she could be found in Jay Cooke State Park. He had given specific directions with roads and landmarks. "You'll find her chained to a tree."

Alice had been dumbfounded, but a few minutes later she had turned the information over to the Minneapolis Police Department.

When Brother de Paul returned to Minneapolis the next day, he was shocked to hear of the kidnapping and the release of Mrs. Piper. He had not heard nor read any news at the retreat house.

The F.B.I. agents swarmed to the Twin Cities questioning neighbors, friends, employees and business associates of the Pipers. They also checked ex-convicts asking them where they were on that Thurday. The agents spent many hours with Brother de Paul seeking his help with names and places.

"As far as the public and the media knew, there was a 'mystery man' who had received the call. . . . I did not want my name revealed in case there were further contacts."

A month later, the Minneapolis Star front page story "Piper kidnapper contact named," told about the call that Alice had received. Brother de Paul was very upset that someone had revealed his identity to the newspaper. He had given much confidential information to the F.B.I. agents and he felt that at least one of them was involved in the "leak" to the press.

The switchboard at the House of Charity was deluged with calls from newspapers, magazines, radio and television stations across the nation. Brother de Paul went off by himself to pray and to think. He decided he would give each of the local television channels, a few radio stations and the Minneapolis Star separate interviews because they had been so helpful to him through the years.

"I can only say why I think the kidnappers called me . . . because of the trust so many inmates, probationers and parolees had in me. Many had confided deep and confidential secrets to me which were and are well kept. I have spent 20 years working with convicts and men with problems. They trust me. The ransom was paid a short distance from the Northside House of Charity and some of it was supposed to be hidden in a junkyard not far from here. These are times of great concern for us."

The police, the detectives and the F.B.I. worked on the Piper kidnapping case for almost five years before two men were indicted. Brother de Paul and Alice were required to testify at their trial; he for the defense and she for the prosecution!

Chapter 42

20 YEARS
of Service to the Needy

This was the 20th anniversary of the founding of the House of Charity on Nicollet Island and now they had only a few months before the dining room would be demolished. Brother de Paul had spent many days searching for a new place. Most of his volunteers warned him, "you'll never move the long line of men off the island." He knew it would be a struggle, but the last 20 years had geared him to accept challenges. It had to be in a central point, accessible to people from all parts of the city.

He found an old warehouse at 7th Street and Park Avenue and once again he had visions that very few others shared. Even though late at night, when he first saw it, he knew it was the place. He had visited about 50 feeding places in the United States and had seen some dismal settings with dirty dishes, dark waiting rooms and people having to stand while eating. The House of Charity would have none of that. This dump of a warehouse would be transformed into an attractive, cheerful, easy-to-clean dining room. Many people, including the Board of Directors, thought a bare minimum of remodeling to pass the fire, safety, health and sanitation inspections would be enough. Brother de Paul insisted, "Just because it's for the poor, it shouldn't be a bare and austere room." To add a touch of class to the new building, he named it the House of Charity Food Centre. The Minneapolis City Council, after much haggling, approved the building to be used as a dining room.

One of the residents, Bob Hopperton, was an all-around handy man and Brother put him to work. The warehouse had several walls that had to be torn down to make one large dining room. The furnace had to be dismantled and a new heating system put in. Brother did more begging for money and for free or discounted panelling, flooring, air conditioning and iron railing. The health department allowed them to move their dishwashing machine, but none of the other old kitchen equipment. The steam kettles, the stoves and the steam tables all had to be new. Brother de Paul had a target date for opening the new Food Centre, Thanksgiving Day.

In the meantime, the 20th Anniversary was celebrated. The Troubadors, volunteers who ran the House of Bargains, had an ecumenical scripture service and a dinner in their honor. The A.A. Group had an Open House and heard encouraging words from Lynn Carroll, a nationally known counselor for alcoholics for over 30 years.

On Sunday, October 1, 1972, 20 priests concelebrated a Mass of Thanksgiving at St. Joseph's Church in North Minneapolis. This majestic old church would also be demolished for the freeway. Each priest represented one year in the life of the House of Charity. The honored guests were the Protestant ministers, Orthodox and Episcopalian priests and Salvation Army officers who had conducted the ecumenical scripture services each Wednesday evening. Residents of the House of Charity joined the St. Joseph's Usher Club to welcome the guests. Music from the grand old pipe organ filled the church before, during and after the Mass. A "hymnfest" of the most popular hymns at the House of Charity was held for a half hour before the church bells announced the 20th anniversary celebration. A trumpet solo echoed throughout as the procession of clergy marched from the rectory to the altar. The Holy Name Church choir plus several soloists lent their talent to make the celebration a loud hallelujah for the House of Charity. Sylvia Little's singing of the Lord's Prayer was unforgettable.

Mark Mallander, a former work trainee, brought greetings from Governor Wendell Anderson who had proclaimed that Sunday "Brother de Paul's House of Charity Day." Then Father R. K. Smith, Rector of St. Patrick's Episcopal Church, known for his delightful humor, represented the "Protestant" community in his greetings. Father Patrick Lannon, the homilist, praised the House of Charity as "people of action." He had just lost a lot of weight and he challenged the congregation: "If I can do the impossible, so can you!"

Brother de Paul needed this support. Although he was convinced that GOD always provided every need, he felt a heavy loss at the thought of leaving his beloved Nicollet Island.

The work on the new dining room was going slowly; there were so many building regulations that had to be followed to pass the inspections. Throughout November, Brother de Paul pushed the workers to finish the Food Centre. After the electricians, the plumbers and the carpenters were through, it still needed to be decorated and furnished. The men and volunteers came in on Saturdays to finish the job. Less than 48 hours before the grand opening on Thanksgiving Eve, when an ecumenical scripture service of thanksgiving was held, the water was turned on.

The last meal was served in the dining room on Nicollet Island on Wednesday, November 26; the first meal in the new Food Centre on Park Avenue was served on Thanksgiving Day, November 27th. Brother de Paul wanted the switch made without stopping his feeding program for even a day. All four television channels showed the opening day complete turkey dinner being served in the warm, bright, newly decorated dining room. Brother de Paul was all smiles as he greeted each guest; this was the culmination of a long search for a new place for "his people" to eat. "His people" exclaimed with "oohs" and "aahs" when they saw the large, beautifully panelled dining room and the sparkling newly equipped kitchen.

On the same day that the Food Centre was opened, the Minnesota Restaurant Association presented Brother de Paul with a copy of a resolution passed by its members. They acknowledged his early concern for the hungry and destitute, his founding the House of Charity feeding program, his moving it from the island to the new Food Centre and his maintaining an unblemished sanitation record. "Be it hereby resolved that the members of the Minnesota Restaurant Association request that the M.R.A. Board of Directors bestow an honorary degree of membership to Brother de Paul and the Food Centre with all rights and privileges of membership."

Brother was touched by this acknowledgement. "Maybe my insistence on cleanliness paid off, even though it took a lot of pressure, direction and sometimes strict words through the years. I know I bug some people when I say, 'Don't go out with dirty windows on your truck. You're representing the House of Charity,' 'Look at this filthy door,' or 'Pick up that garbage.' I always want to offer our guests a dignified and clean place to eat. I had to do a lot of pushing, hollering, demanding, hiring and firing to accomplish this.

"We have a fantastic man in charge of the dining room now, Don Lebak. He's responsible for the high '99' mark we got from the sanitation inspector. Even though his crew has not always been stable, he has prepared and served delicious and nutritious meals with dignity and caring."

Shortly after Brother de Paul opened the new Food Centre, he was surprised and thrilled to receive the DeLaSalle Alumni Award. At the banquet, he told the audience about his early years at DeLaSalle High School on Nicollet Island. "I saw the poor and alcoholics without anyone or

TWO OF THE MANY GUESTS who came to the FOOD CENTRE — Millions of hot, nourishing, tasty meals have been served gratis.

LOOKING AT ONE OF THE MANY TURKEYS being prepared for the holiday guests at the Food Centre — Brother de Paul checks it out with Don Lebak, manager, and one of the cooks.

ENJOYING A VISIT — the founder was at the Food Centre daily when possible . . . he loves to go table to table joking with the hungry guests, many of whom he knows by first names.

any place to go. I knew I wanted to do something, but I didn't know what. I learned that a person couldn't be concerned merely with DeLaSalle or just his own church. There are many others who desperately need to be shown God's love. . . . I really liked it a lot at De. I think one of the best things was the tough discipline we got from the Brothers."

Brother de Paul remembered his austere high school days when he received a letter from Father Tom Peichel of Holy Trinity Church in Winsted, Minnesota with a check for $50. Father wrote, "We just had a special Lenten mass with our kids in the high school and part of the offering was a collection of money. When we presented them with a list of needs and causes, including your House of Charity, they voted to send it to you.

"We would like to follow this up and let them know what the money will do for the House of Charity. We would also like to give them more incentive to give to this need and needs in general."

Brother de Paul was happy to write to these generous students at Holy Trinity High School. He thanked them, explained his feeding, clothing and housing of God's poor, and he invited them to visit the new Food Centre next time they were in Minneapolis.

Answering letters had become a daily contact with the world for Brother. About 10:00 p.m. after he had finished his other duties, he would read letters from local contributors, from people who appreciated his daily telephone messages, from prisoners, from shut-ins all over the United States and from friends all over the world. Each letter writer received a personal, typewritten note from Brother de Paul. Sometimes the resident in the room below lay awake half the night listening to the peck-pecking of the typewriter.

Easter that spring was special again as residents and guests gathered on the porch of the Northside House of Charity for their Easter Sunrise Service. They heard the gospel story of the Resurrection and sang Allelujahs.

All day Brother de Paul shared his time with residents of a nursing home, men and women in the city jail and the hundreds of people who came to eat at the Food Centre.

At 6:00 p.m. the chapel was filled with residents, benefactors, volunteers and friends as the Easter Trumpet Service began. The trumpet announced the grand entrance of a live Paschal lamb. Everyone loved the services as they were warm, friendly, and a lot of expressions of love, and hugging. Especially on holidays did lonely people find comfort and fellowship.

Dr. David Preus, national Bishop of the American Lutheran Church, was the guest speaker. When he saw the Easter lilies surrounding the altar, he said, "They are like trumpets announcing the resurrection."

He also told the community "The House of Charity is one of the most well-known and respected places in the city. It stands as a monument with the IDS Tower and the Guthrie Theater to all the people of this city, but for a different reason — its exceptional love of and service to the forgotten poor.''

Chapter 43

Just as there was opposition to the House of Charity when it was started on Nicollet Island and again when it moved to the North side of Minneapolis, some of the neighbors for five or six blocks around the new Food Centre complained about the "line-up." The hungry started queuing outside the building about a half hour before the doors opened. Mostly men, but the number of women would increase as the end of the month drew near and their income of welfare ran out. The women and children waited inside.

When any one of the men heard the complaints and relayed them to Brother de Paul, he assured them that "we must use time to win them over. It worked before and I'm sure it will work here."

Many of the guests at the House of Charity Food Centre brought containers or plastic bags which they filled with any left-overs. This was their supper or weekend meal. Whenever there was a good supply of bakery goods, the rolls, bread and doughnuts were put in large white plastic containers and wheeled to a spot by the exit door. Each person could help himself.

When Brother de Paul realized the House of Charity's savings account balance was over $100,000 after the mortgage was paid on the Food Centre, he felt that they should find new charities and begin tithing. Soon they would get $271,000 from the Minnesota Highway Department for their Northside residence. He didn't favor begging for more money with this large bank account unless he looked for more people in need. He found them — the starving, the homeless all over the world. Their plight touched Brother just as the hungry in Minneapolis had for more than twenty years. He would beg for them.

Brother de Paul on the advice of a long time clergy friend, hadn't attended a board meeting in a long time, but with his "right arm," Alice Codden, and Lillian Halvorsen, the president of the Good Samaritan League, Brother went to the board meeting on October 11, 1973 and announced that he had incorporated an overseas food relief agency.

The board members were stunned. When one asked Alice why he did this, "You all drove him to it," she explained. "You have a different philosophy about the House of Charity. You're not sympathetic with his approach. You base everything on a secular, business level; he tries to base everything on trust in God."

The board members were concerned that the founder would not raise money for the local work.

The fall bazaar and dinner in 1973 was held for the new non-profit feeding organization, the first of many fund raisers to help feed the poor of the world.

Brother de Paul had always felt a strong desire to feed the hungry and he wanted no boundaries now in feeding these people. "A hungry person needs to be fed because he is hungry."

With the residence in one location on the northside and the dining room in another, downtown, it was difficult for Brother de Paul to be available for all the phone calls. People with problems called almost every day. Many people just wanted to talk to him.

He announced a telephone number they could call to put their petitions on the "Prayer Board." Then Brother, the residents, staff and volunteers remembered them in their prayers in the Ecumenical Chapel. Sisters in Osaka, Japan, among many in the world, prayed each day for anyone calling on the PRAYER BOARD.

He also decided he would put an inspirational message on tape and when anyone called, they would hear his words of inspiration, of encouragement, of humor, of information, of advice, of healing and of love. The first day, October 19, 1973 there were 58 calls. He taped these messages whenever and wherever he had the time — in his office, in jails, on airplanes, in the Holy Land and even in the Chicago Stock Exchange. A new message every day without fail!!

Chapter 44

Early in 1974, Brother de Paul made his first visit to Vietnam, Korea and India to see where he could be most helpful. A friend bought his plane ticket and he stayed with Missionary Brothers of Charity. The starving and desperately poor, especially mothers and children, tugged at his heart. He decided that his new overseas relief agency would financially "adopt" a home for destitute mothers and orphaned children in Saigon, Vietnam. It was a small house with 70 children crowded into it, operated by the Missionary Brothers of Charity. The Vietnamese had been fighting for years and some were unable to take care of their families; many were killed, leaving widows and orphans. There were many orphans fathered by American servicemen.

When Brother returned to Minneapolis and realized once again how much material wealth the House of Charity enjoyed, he wrote to each board member:

"This is one of the most urgent letters I have ever written to you. There are millions of persons, our brothers and sisters in Christ, who are suffering to the extent that countless numbers die each day of starvation.

"In all of the years, we have had the BUILDING FUND (our savings account) I have never consented to withdraw money for anything but that of purchasing, remodeling, and equipping whatever building was in need of it during our many changes of locations. I worked hard to raise the funds needed for other expenses without touching the building fund. I am thoroughly convinced that we should send more than $10,000.00 through ecumenical relief agencies — to help feed the starving persons abroad. I realize that it is a small "dent" but everywhere men *must* begin with any amounts so that something can be done to alleviate this suffering.

"As followers of JESUS, we cannot sleep peacefully at night, knowing that so many people suffer . . . for over 22 years we have worked hard to alleviate that suffering locally . . . it is very late, but at least we can redeem ourselves now.

"As followers of JESUS, we must break through customs, traditions, and bureaucratic procedures to help alleviate this suffering which is almost unbelievable. To delay any further would, in my opinion, betray our Christian trust as persons and as members of the board of the House of Charity.

"It might be that this witness to our beliefs might encourage others, too, to look realistically and compassionately at such horrible suffering on such a big scale. What good are buildings — or anything for that matter — when a human person suffers such degradation. To have money in the bank as we do and not help at this crucial hour in the history of mankind, would be to refuse the request for help from JESUS himself.

"The starving of the world haunt us — and our prayers and practices must be matched with a comparable amount of sacrifice and concern.

"GOD will take care of our needs as HE has for over 22 years if we do our part!!

"Thank you for your prompt and prayerful consideration — and you might want to add your own personal sacrifices."

—Brother de Paul

Three board members gave prompt and agreeable consideration to Brother's letter, seven abstained. The Good Samaritan League sent a letter to each board member telling them of their unanimous vote of support for sending $10,000 to the poor of the world. One board member recommended sending $20,000.00. Owen Beckwith, the president, talked to a clergyman and prayed much before he was convinced that the House of Charity should share in other places in the world.

At the next board meeting in October, 1974, the members debated about the overseas gift. They felt they were custodians of the benefactors' money; would they be breaking their trust? But they discussed and discussed and finally but reluctantly voted to approve of the overseas contribution.

While this meeting was going on, the founder, always eager to learn more and expand his views, attitudes, and experiences, was in Garden Grove, California attending Dr. Robert Schuller's Christian Leadership Institute. Dr. Schuller of television "Hour of Power" fame is one of the founder's heroes. "His philosophy is in the 5 F's which he advocates: Friendly, Firm, Fair, Frank, and Faithful. They helped change my life and helped me, too, to mature in my relationship with others.

"It was a genuine privilege to have lunch with Dr. Schuller. He's warm, affable, kind, thoughtful and a great listener. So many so-called celebrities I have met are different 'off stage,' but not Dr. Schuller. He told me this during lunch, 'I recently received a post card from Mother Teresa; just think a sinner getting a card from a saint!' The warmth and helpfulness of all who work with him in this big organization were a real inspiration to me during my visit. His 'possibility thinking' and doing things big for God influenced my thinking and my actions. He helped me get out of more mental ghettos. Without his influence in my life, I don't know where I would be." The founder was the first Catholic to attend this leadership institute.

It may have been Dr. Schuller's influence that prompted Brother de Paul's action on the following Christmas Day. Jack Olson, of the Northside House of Charity, was in charge of the Christmas cans put in restaurants to let the general public share in helping the House of Charity help others. A car rental company donated a car for the founder's holiday use. He picked up the containers but didn't return. At first, Brother thought Jack might have been mugged. He and Gary Bonin, who had come to help out for three or four days and stayed for years, looked for him until 2:00 a.m. Christmas Day. Everyone's thoughts were on Jack. The car was found abandoned in Peoria, Illinois; and Jack was at the Lighthouse Mission there. Brother de Paul flew to Peoria; Jack left one hour before he arrived. Like the Good Shepherd, Brother wanted Jack to bring the car back to Minneapolis and settle the matter. He has heard from Jack, but he hasn't made any restitution. The founder himself has never owned or driven an automobile.

Five months after their meeting, the Board of Directors approved the withdrawal of $20,000 from the building fund to be used to feed the starving people overseas. $5,000 was given to Care, Inc., a non-denominational social agency that distributes food throughout the world. $5,000 went to Catholic Relief Services. Brother de Paul brought $5,000 to Father McVeigh, director of Catholic Relief Services in Saigon, to help the starving and abandoned refugees on the island of PhuQuoc. The remaining $5,000 Brother took with him to give to Mother Teresa for the destitute and hungry.

While he was in Saigon to dedicate a new and larger home for the children, the North Vietnamese captured the outskirts of the city and people had to get out fast. Brother de Paul used some of the money he had with him to help with their escape. He carried a shopping bag with money on the bottom, produce from the market on top. Most of these people had met Brother de Paul when they had come to Minneapolis for heart surgery under PACT (Persons in Action for Children Today). The Missionary Brothers were part of Mother Teresa's congregation. When Saigon fell, they gave Brother de Paul all their official papers to take to India.

Brother de Paul was stranded in Saigon for a week before he could get a plane out. When he arrived at the Bangkok, Thailand airport the past week's fright, the tension and the danger all bunched up on him and he cried

"NOODLE MAN" — *name given to the founder because of all the tons of food he ships abroad. He stirs noodles cooking in school kitchen in overseas slum.*

A MOMENT OF COURAGE — Brother de Paul attempts a smile when a 75 pound python is wrapped around him in Bangkok.

like a baby. He had held up so well living through the hellish week, "now I just had to let go."

He telephoned Alice, his secretary, in Minneapolis and, although they had a poor connection, he was able to let her know he was safe. His anxious mother was deeply relieved when Alice called her.

When Brother de Paul met Mother Teresa in Calcutta, he was overwhelmed by her simplicity. Her plain Indian sari and her face filled with creases were part of her ordinariness, but her eyes and her heart were filled with love. As they had breakfast together, she told him about the work she and her sisters were doing in Bangladesh for the "poorest of the poor." Both she and Brother firmly believed that "God would provide." When she gave him Holy Communion, he considered it one of the great privileges of his entire life time.

By noon, she had enlisted his help and by evening he was on a plane to Bangladesh. Bangladesh had been East Pakistan and it broke away from West Pakistan in 1971. Since then, millions died of starvation, millions were killed by the Pakistanis who destroyed their homes, their livestock and their tools — and drought, hurricanes and floods devastated their land. When he arrived in Dacca, Bangladesh, he saw the ruins of the sisters' orphanage that had collapsed a few days before he arrived. He promised the sisters to help rebuild.

Brother de Paul confessed, "I was shocked when I arrived in Dacca. It's a steamy, repulsive slum with clotted sewage and garbage everywhere. About one in 10 persons is homeless. Leprosy is common. Malnutrition is the #1 problem."

Brother used his expertise in begging and paid for four large tents from World War II. These were soon filled with boys, ages five to twelve, who were picked up on the street corners, alleys and highways. They had been abandoned and were starving. This makeshift home for the "angels with dirty faces" was rather officially called "The Boys Town of Bangladesh."

When Brother got home, the overseas feeding agency sent funds, desperately needed to feed these boys and to the portable feeding stations that fed the many starving people in this poor country referred to by the U.N. as a "hell hole." He also begged for money to build a decent home for the Boys Town. The tents would not survive when the monsoons came.

When Brother de Paul returned home, he was exhausted, but he sat at his desk to check the mail and his schedule. His eyes rested on a small note tucked into the frame of his blotter. "Dr. Spano died." Alice had known what a shock this would be to Brother, so she tried to announce it as unobtrusively as possible.

"Dr. Spano dead? I can't believe it! O, GOD, rest his soul." Dr. Spano had been his friend, his support on the Board of Directors through all the years of Roncalli House. Dr. Spano had come to all the benefits and functions and knew many of the residents at the House of Charity. He had paid Brother de Paul's travel expenses and had gone with him to visit halfway houses for parolees before they organized the International Halfway House Association. He had been a generous contributor and had obtained contributions and services from others. Brother would sorely miss him as a friend, a confidante, a father-figure.

It seemed that when God took one friend, He supplied another. Mae Moore had moved to Waverly, Minnesota from New York City. One Sunday she read in her church bulletin that the high school kids were collecting food to feed the hungry at the House of Charity in Minneapolis. She donated some canned goods and she asked the young people about the place that feeds the hungry. The next time she took a bus into Minneapolis, she called the House of Charity. "Please put my name in your file. I'd like to be a part of your work." She sent $100 one month, then $200. She kept this up for a year. Then, one day she called Brother de Paul and said, "I think it's time we meet. I'm getting older and can't stand the Minnesota winters, so I'm moving to Florida. Why don't you come out to Waverly to see me?"

When Brother de Paul arrived at her home, he met a very simple, unpretentious, beautiful woman. She told him she was so pleased that the House of Charity was feeding the hungry without preaching to them.

Brother told Mae about the remodeling that was being done on the new downtown building. She gave him a check for $10,000.

When Mae moved to Florida, Brother found someone to pack her delicate china for the trip.

Shortly after she was settled, she became ill. Her niece found her unconscious on the floor of her apartment and several days later, she died. She left her entire estate, $78,000 to the House of Charity. Brother received a letter from one of her nieces saying how thrilled they were that their aunt was so concerned about the poor. There was no jealousy nor contesting of the will. Brother de Paul believed it was the providence of God, once again, that brought Mae Moore to the House of Charity through the high school kids' food collection.

All through the years, God seemed to have placed people who were helpful and encouraging in Brother de Paul's life. Some were celebrities, some were his own "little people." Among the former was Bob Montgomery, known on WCCO radio as Bob White. Brother knew him during DeLaSalle High School days when Bob was a streetcar conductor to help pay his own tuition. He interviewed Brother on WCCO radio to help the House of Charity become better known. He put together shows at Stillwater Prison and he emceed some of the Charity Dinners. When Bob went to work for the Christopher Movement in New York, he remained a faithful benefactor and friend. One time when Brother de Paul was in New

York, Bob introduced him to Father Keller, the founder of the Christophers. Long ago, Brother had been influenced by Father Keller's work in bringing Christ to the marketplace and now he was thrilled to have met and visited with this man, who inspired millions of people to make the world a better place.

Howard Viken, also of WCCO radio fame, whose morning programs are considered to have the biggest listening audience of the day, has been a generous benefactor, too. He has interviewed Brother many times. Once, as he talked to Brother de Paul before he left for Bangladesh, Howard wrote him a check right on the air. Thousands of dollars were raised for his overseas feeding program as a result of the interview. Many times when Brother sends Howard Viken postcards from overseas, they are shared with his listening audience.

Another friend, John Gallos, a well-known television star, has featured Brother de Paul and his work, making him better known to many viewers in the Twin City area. He has shown slides of Brother's overseas travels and has brought many contributors into the "fold."

These and many more friends seem to have been at the right place at the right time — Brother de Paul thought it was God's providence.

Chapter 45

After the Minnesota Highway Department paid for the House of Charity building on the northside, the need to find a new location became much more intense. Several downtown locations were investigated, but Brother de Paul felt they should stay on the northside of Minneapolis. He felt their housing and emergency services were needed in that area of the city.

When no prospects for a northside location appeared and a very appealing one near the downtown Food Centre was offered, Brother de Paul thought he must change his mind. The Field Hotel at 510 South 8th Street was for sale. It had been used as a residence for blind people, but the number living there had dwindled since the blind had become more independent.

It was a large building, four stories high with 110 rooms. Brother saw possibilities of knocking a wall out here to make a meeting room, knocking out a few walls there to make a chapel, a dining room and a lounge, and enlarging the kitchen. Yes, with a lot of remodeling, it would make a suitable House of Charity. They had to get the approval of the Minneapolis City Council, which they did on May 14, 1976, before the sale was complete. For $300,000, Brother de Paul had his fourth home for the House of Charity. The owner of the hotel donated all the furniture to the new owners.

Besides receiving prayer petitions for the chapel bulletin board each day and recording his Daily Inspirational messages which by now had received over 300,000 calls, Brother de Paul began a weekly radio program called Mission of Mercy. Each Wednesday evening's Ecumenical Service, where people from many backgrounds and denominations came together to

FOURTH HOUSE OF CHARITY is in downtown Minneapolis on South 8th Street.

worship, was recorded and later aired on several radio stations around the state on Saturday afternoon and Sunday evening.

"From Minneapolis, Minnesota, the Mission of Mercy, a non-profit organization presents the weekly broadcast, 'Mission of Mercy' . . . an opportunity to reach out our hands and grasp the hands of others of various faiths, to worship, to break down the high walls of denominationalism and to reach out with hearts and hands to the degraded, the miserable and the hungry around the world."

Part of the program each week was the "Lord's Prayer Around the World." The Lord's Prayer was said in different languages to emphasize the theme that God's love reaches out to people of all nationalities, cultures and backgrounds. Every country in Europe, many in Africa, the Mideast, Southeast Asia and Latin America were represented in this weekly prayer. It was an ecumenical pilgrimage from people all around the world to his interfaith chapel.

Brother de Paul received many thank you notes from people who listened to his daily messages and his radio program. One 92-year old wrote: "I enjoy your service so much on Sundays. It's such a blessing to me. I have a bad hip and can't get to church." Another woman said, "Listened to your radio program last night and can hardly believe such ecumenical things are really going on here in Minneapolis. You're friends with all denominations and it's really working out."

One woman wrote to thank him as "a God-given friend via 'Ma Bell,'" whose voice brought many, many messages that were especially applicable to me. Your beautiful voice is there in the middle of the night when my mind is heavy and filled with anxiety, fears of the future and reflections of the past."

Another woman told him, "I had my entire family listen to your message yesterday because it really struck home!"

A man wrote: "We recently bought a telephone amplifier and now, at the end of our evening meal, my entire family of seven enjoys your messages and discusses their relationship to our lives."

The daily messages had been recorded for three years and now the calls were so numerous it required four telephones to take care of them.

The Bicentennial year was celebrated all over the United States, all over the world, really. Brother de Paul had visited the Mt. Olivet School in Seoul, Korea several times and his over seas organization had given the school various gifts. This year he had provided radio repair equipment for the students. He was surprised and overwhelmed when he received a large wooden carving from the teachers and students at the school. It was an American eagle, hand-carved by the students, "your bicentennial gift from us." This school had been founded by Rev. Reuben Youngdahl of Mt. Olivet Church in Minneapolis and Brother felt honored to represent the church five times in Korea, on his trips to Thailand and Bangladesh. It was very difficult for Brother to hold back his tears when he was made HONORARY principal of the Korean school.

Seven Protestant churches near the Food Centre organized a series of "Good Neighbor Fellowship Rallies" to celebrate the Bicentennial and they invited Brother de Paul to be the speaker at the first one. A great Bicentennial Singspiration was held in the Augustana Lutheran Church parking lot with hymns and patriotic songs and with special music by the Rainbow Group from Findley College in Ohio.

Brother felt more accepted now in the downtown area and he was happy that the House of Charity would soon be moving there.

It took the residents and volunteers a month, in the heat of the summer, to move the House of Charity from the Northside of Minneapolis to 510 South 8th Street. They used the two House of Bargains trucks which carried the message "We're loaded with bargains" and the food truck's logo which was even more appropos with their new location, "Heart of the City."

Several men wrapped blankets around the statue of Christ and rode with it to the new home. Because it had faded and peeled and had to be repainted several times, the Good Samaritan League spent over $4,000 to make a suitable curved, moisture-proof, heat-proof, cold-proof, tinted glass enclosure for the statue of Christ. With two spotlights illuminating the window, the House of Charity was still "the place in Minneapolis that has Christ in the window."

The remodeling went on slowly. About nine rooms had to be knocked out on the first floor for the chapel. Brother de Paul designed the beautiful chapel with wood ceiling beams, carpeting and stained glass windows. One of the windows had loaves and fishes depicting the constant miracle Christ is performing with food in the Food Centre. Another portrayed a black hand and a white hand clasped in prayer; and the ecumenical window showed an Orthodox, a Celtic and a Christian cross entwined as one cross. These stained glass windows were made possible by the Mission of Mercy for use in this chapel. The residents asked if they could help and were so proud of the window they bought with money they had saved for years to buy a pool table! New pews were also available as a memorial in the ecumenical chapel for $195 each. No names were displayed; all memorials are known to GOD.

The cost of the remodeling job was overwhelming with inflation boosting the price of labor and materials. The first winter's fuel bills in such a large building were overpowering to the founder who always tried to keep bills currently paid.

Once again, he turned to his benefactors. Due to the energy crisis, the annual St. Patrick's Day benefit dinner could not be held in the church hall as usual. The heat was turned down right after school hours. After much thought and prayer Brother decided to ask for gifts instead of having the dinner. He sold tickets for a cash prize and drew the winner's name in the Alice Codden lobby on St. Patrick's Day.

Because many of the residents at the new House of Charity were elderly or handicapped, it was difficult for them to walk the steps. An elevator shaft was added to the outside of the building to help them get to the upper floors. This addition was "topped" with a cross to tell the whole city "what we stand for and what we're here for, to love and serve people." The license inspector wanted the huge lighted cross to be licensed but Brother would not accept that — the cross was a religious symbol, not a commercial sign.

Earlier this year, Brother de Paul made his fourth mission of mercy, his third to Bangladesh. Each time he wondered where his plane fare and needed supplies would come from, but they always came. "God never turns me down," he explained.

Before he left, he was given a community send-off with clergy from seven denominations. "I feel the strength and support of priests and ministers of many faiths when I kneel for their blessings. Each is intoned in a different custom, tradition and language as they invoke God's blessing on our work for the poor of the world."

The new ecumenical chapel was ready for the traditional Holy Week and Easter services. With the lilies around the new altar, the stained glass windows and the new pews, it was a gorgeous setting for worship; it lifted the spirit of many.

A few weeks later, Alice Codden, his secretary for 22 years, organized a birthday scripture service in the new chapel for Brother de Paul's 48th birthday. In her letter to his friends and benefactors she wrote, "Wherever people are hurting, hungry and helpless materially and spiritually, he is there!" With pictures of him surrounded by kids in Bangladesh, she called him a modern "Pied Piper." He "adored" kids everywhere.

The 25th anniversary of Brother de Paul's founding of the House of Charity caused him to reflect on what had been accomplished with 25¢ and God. From the seven room house in Northeast Minneapolis, to 17 years of pioneering on Nicollet Island, to the seven hopeful years on the Northside and finally to their first year in their big new home in downtown Minneapolis, all seemed like a dream.

It had been a long, tough, unbelievable, often very discouraging road to travel, but Brother and his associates had found a lot of joy and had felt it a privilege to assist their brothers and sisters in need. They had come a tremendous way from the days when they all slept on the floor with no heat and little to eat.

The celebration began with a special Wednesday evening service on July 13, 1977, in the new air-conditioned chapel with their long time friend and benefactor Bishop Paul Dudley as the speaker. Another Wednesday evening service honored the Troubadors for their dedicated work in the House of Bargains. Still another Wednesday, everyone gathered to honor Alice Codden on her 77th birthday. She had devoted the last 22 years as office manager and Christmas gift organizer with no count of the hours she'd worked. "Brother Alice's" friends presented her with a trip to Phoenix and the lobby at the new House of Charity was dedicated to her and called "Alice Codden Lobby." She chose the words that were hung under her photograph: "Ask God's blessing on your work, but do not also ask Him to do it." It fitted her perfectly.

Banners were draped across the front of the four-story House of Charity and the Food Centre announcing the 25th year, "Let us thank God for these fantastic years of service!" A lighted sign identifying Brother de Paul's

House of Charity was hung on the front of the building. The bottom half of the sign carried a weekly message and the first week Brother de Paul's three favorite words were inscribed: "God Love You." Each week Brother used a quotation or made up one of his own. During election week: "Vote, or else do not complain." A favorite was "No coffin ever had pockets."

In the middle of January he tried to find solace, "Without the winter, how could we know spring?" People who drove by the House of Charity frequently told the founder they looked for the new message every week.

On Sunday, October 2nd at two o'clock in the afternoon, a mass of thanksgiving was concelebrated at Our Lady of Lourdes Church, which had been nearby the House of Charity when it was located on Nicollet Island. Clergymen of various faiths who had been associated with the House of Charity, the founder's relatives, past and present residents, staff and volunteers, auxiliary members, friends and benefactors gathered with Brother de Paul to thank GOD for all of HIS blessings. They came from all over the United States, from Canada and Korea, to join an unusually spirited and enthusiastic worship. The festive and united singing by the visiting choirs and congregation made this a liturgical celebration which many remembered for a long, long time.

The old church thundered twice with applause. Once when the founder thanked everyone, reviewed the past 25 years and his philosophy. And again when he went over to give Alice, his faithful secretary, a peck on the cheek. Everyone in this longest consecutively used house of worship in Minneapolis was thrilled to be there in such an atmosphere of real gratitude for this silver anniversary. Everyone, too, felt like part of "one big family." The founder's mother and father sat proudly in the front pew.

FOUNDER AS A BABY — Alice Codden, the founders' secretary, hangs his baby photo, on the occasion of his 50th birthday.

BISHOP PAUL DUDLEY chats with Alice Codden at the 25th anniversary celebration at the entrance to the interfaith chapel in July of 1977.

During the unusual homily, which was shared by five clergymen, Reverend J. Millard Ahlstrom, a close Lutheran friend, read with great feeling an ode he had written for this special occasion.

While Brother de Paul was helping with the distribution of Communion, his youngest sister, Vonnie, stood before him with a beautiful smile and tears of happiness in her eyes. As he offered her the host, saying "Body of Christ, Vonnie," he was overwhelmed with love and the memory of her 25 years ago, when she had thrown her arms around him and had asked, "When are you coming home, Tommy?" For a moment he stopped, held the ciborium in his left hand, patted her cheek with his right hand and said, "Vonnie, love you." Her question 25 years ago tied in with the initial struggle Brother had to continue his work. Now it was a re-dedication of what God wanted him to do.

To tell the story of the House of Charity from the time Brother de Paul first conceived the idea of helping the poor, through the many years of struggle to get his program going, until the happy 25th anniversary celebration, Terry Studanski, the Mission of Mercy radio producer, filmed a 17-minute movie in living color, called "25¢ and God."

Brother de Paul began the narration about his goals in starting to feed the hungry by quoting Mahatma Ghandi, "To the hungry, God comes in the form of bread."

Dick Hulan, formerly Brother Francis, came for the anniversary and in the movie he reminisced about the time the man had come to turn off their electricity. Brother de Paul and the other Brothers had rushed to the chapel to pray and when they finished, a benefactor was at the door with a donation. "That's how Brother operated then, and that's how he operates now; solely on faith that God will provide."

The movie reviewed Brother's visits to the prisons and jails on holidays where he reached through the bars to clasp the inmates' hands, give them a smile and a personal gift. Brother de Paul told of the valuable volunteers who helped make the House of Charity work, of Alice Codden, his secretary for the past 22 years, "who has shared so tremendously, so intimately, so entirely in the things we do at the House of Charity."

With her ready smile, Alice explained, "It's been a real privilege for me to work with Brother, and as I stayed on year after year, I felt in my heart I could never leave." There were scenes of Brother de Paul's "Operation Noodle" in Haiti, where the shipments of noodles had been the only food available to many families.

The movie ended with the Reverend Ahlstrom reading the ode he had written for Brother de Paul on the 25th anniversary.

Lines Inscribed for the Twenty-Fifth Anniversary of the House of Charity
October 2, 1977

Far cry from the glistening marble
Of the floating dome of St. Peter's,
The Swiss Guards in gaudy garb,
The mystique and magnificence of the Holy City,
Center of our august and catholic Faith:

Nicollet Island a long shout from all of that:
Tawdry saloons, squalid leaning brick:
There in bleakness and decrepitude
A decade ago I found the House of Charity,
And found a man, Brother de Paul,
And his surrogate, "Mrs. Bishop," Alice Codden.

Found a three-storied refuge of the dispossessed,
Flanked by rinkydink neon signs of bars,
Fronting on traffic of the avenue
And the blowing scraps of littered paper,
Standing there a sentinel of sobriety and refuge,
With the white-fronted dining room
Clean-shining across the street,
And the man in the alb
Greeting the long shuffling line
As they entered to dine in dignity.

There in that place I baptized one Gus Yaeger
In the solemn passage of Holy Week,
Gus, a wisp of spirit bound from Whence to Whither;
Met Louie, Don, and others whose names elude me now;
Reuben the cook (mud turtle man from Alexandria);
Willie Davis, large, black, gentle,
Thirty years in Society's ugly warehouse,
Doing penitence in dungeons for murder,
Now out to look around a bit, and then to die:
Buried we him in pauper's casket.

Sylvia Little singing, votive lights aflicker;
At Easter, nuns and all of us jumping
As we pricked the banging balloons;

Always the incongruous Jesus-statue
Looking on benignly;
Always Alice, always Brother de Paul.

What chance this Quixotic hope?
One man against the lost and terrifying world,
Unmitred, without the bishop's ring,
He with the tin cup begging,
He with handful of tatterdemalions,
Sans prestigious foundations,
No pipeline to the thrones of power:
How shall he mitigate a hungry world,
How stanch a million bleeding wounds?

Brother, you shout forth splendid futility:
Feed three hundred,
And a million bloat their bellies starving;
Hold hands in circle breathing love,
While lurking hate flaunts peace,
And megatons await unleashing.

But on this glad natal day of the House of love
("Hogtidlighet" we say in Swedish),
I bring my alms to you, and all my love,
And sing my paean of praise.

You with your badges of charity,
Puny, pitted against the Beast,
Remind me a little of Calvary,
Ill matched against the Caesar:
And yet, five wounds
By the garbage pits of Jerusalem
Can match the whole wide world.

Just so the House of Charity holds the Cross against the sun,
Betting that love shall overcome,
That the cup of water to the thirsty,
The bread to the one who hungers,
Does bear the imprimatur of God.

J. Millard Ahlstrom

Chapter 46

For almost 26 years Brother de Paul had suffered what he called "the early morning syndrome." It was an anxiety that had become deep seated through the years and was always with him. As he awoke each morning the questions leaped at him. Would the cook be there today? Or would he become intoxicated during the night? Would the drivers show up? The truck used for picking up food could be parked in the middle of an intersection, abandoned, while the driver goes to get a drink. Would someone come in to answer the telephone? To keep the place clean? Sometimes it took 40 people to keep the operation of the House of Charity and the Food Centre going. No one was permanent. Most of the men had long histories of drinking, instability and emotional problems and they needed constant supervision. Many of them became dependable workers; many of them didn't.

Brother de Paul became adept at substituting quickly, but the stress inside was always there, wearing him down. "There are beautiful people in my life who've shared this anxiety. Alice Codden is always there when I need her. The Troubadors, who run the stores, some of the staff, the auxiliaries and volunteers understand the daily stress I'm under."

Besides the ever-present anxiety, the daily phone message, the weekly radio program and the starving people in Bangladesh and Haiti, all took their toll on Brother's physical and emotional health. He had struggled with weariness, discouragement, pain and agony and after 26 years, he was physically, emotionally, mentally and spiritually worn out. He had to be revitalized.

Since Brother saw his first mountain in 1949, he has been awestruck by their strength. They seemed to reach out to God and lift his spirit. He had read in Psalm 121, "I look to the mountains, where will my help come from? My help comes from the Lord, Who made heaven and earth." That was what he needed now — to go to the mountain. Throughout history, mountains have been the site of God's work. Abraham had taken Isaac to Mt. Marish to offer him as a sacrifice when the Lord intervened. On Mt. Sinai, the Lord gave Moses the 10 Commandments and the transfiguration took place on Mt. Thabor.

With money he'd received from a special friend, he flew to his favorite shrines in the mountains, Fatima and Lourdes. From here he wrote to his staff, his family, and his friends to tell them where he was and why. He asked them to pray for him; he was searching for God to give him more strength to cope with the problems of the last few years. He told them that he needed each one of them. "I know I come across as being self-sufficient, — to a degree I am, but I need God and I need you. Sometimes I feel I am always begging and pleading for your help. I need you to share in this work as a team or a family. I can't do this alone. God is using me, for some strange reason, as an instrument in this great work of His, but I need you. I need our benefactors. I need the people we serve. I need my own blood family. Support me as I go up to the mountain. When I come back, please be there with your arms outstretched and with your assurance that you are with me."

He went to the mountain to pray and had some of the most beautiful prayer days of his life. He reviewed his 26 years at the House of Charity and the five years overseas. He struggled and prayed and meditated about his life and opened his heart like never before. "What had I done with God's help? What does He want me to do now?"

Brother prayed through the days and into the nights, outdoors under the stars and even in the rain. The mountains seemed to hold the grandeur and majesty of God, but when Brother remembered the biblical verse from Psalm 97, "The mountains melt like wax before the Lord, before the Lord of all the earth," he was conscious of only one thing. The most important job for him and for everyone was to save one's immortal soul. "To be with God forever is the only thing that counts in our whole life," he later told the listeners to his daily message. "I have not solved all of my problems, much of the dilemma remains, but I know what must be retained, what must be changed and what new direction God wants from me in my life. I'm down from the mountain. Pray for me."

At a seminar entitled, "Let's never forget where we came from" a few months later, Brother de Paul recounted the history of their work. He told how, with 25¢ and God, the House of Charity had grown from the little house on 2nd Street Northeast to the two large buildings downtown. These buildings were a testimony to all the hard work, the struggles, the faith and the love that were present through the 26 years.

With no guaranteed income, Brother de Paul told them he always had financial problems. "When you get into a tight pinch, I think God is trying to see if we really trust Him." The House of Charity bank account was usually overdrawn until the Christmas appeal donations came in. Thousands of people who care have supported the House of Charity because they trusted Brother and his staff.

Then he talked about "volunteers who come in very enthusiastic about working and changing things. They don't realize there have been years of experimenting, research. Many trials, many errors, but also many successes. I am the founder. In the eyes of God and man, that puts a unique responsibility on me. It's like bringing a child into the world, and each of you, as staff, has come to help me rear that child. . . .

"Being a pioneer, you do not always find people who agree with you and support you. Many times it's the people close to you who oppose you.

"We came from a difficult start. We had to push and pull, knock, scream and holler, demand, fire and re-hire to maintain standards of dignity and love.

"I've heard some of you say, 'It's so difficult to communicate with Brother de Paul.' First of all, I am a human being. I'm not flawless. I get angry when someone says, 'Boy, is Brother hard to talk to.' It's usually because they are not open with me. When you want dialogue with me, it's got to be frank and honest. You may not always get the answer when you want it, but I hear you."

Brother de Paul recounted the fund raising events, the dinners, the bazaars, the festivals, and rummage sales that the auxiliaries, the staff, the volunteers and the residents worked so hard on. "Now we have no events; we have letters that go out to thousands of people at Christmas, St. Patrick's Day and in mid-summer asking for financial help. In the 20th century, it's good for people to know they are the answer to the House of Charity's trust in God. They are men and women who love God through helping people, and the House of Charity is people.

"We have to have a team spirit — the bookkeeper, the mailroom clerk, the switchboard operator, the drivers, Miss Codden, the Food Centre staff, the volunteers at the store and myself. We have to work together. Each one is important. We have to respect each person's time. Don't call the Food Centre during the lunch hour. If I'm tired and cranky, don't press. Use your judgment, your sensitivity. I do get days of pressure and I try to be careful when you have them."

Then he told the staff about one of the most diffucult times in his life — when he had "to go to the mountain" last summer. "I thank those of you who did such a beautiful job while I was gone. I left with a lot of doubt, but I came back strengthened by God's grace. We can go on and do great things with His help and with each other. We are all holding hands, but if one breaks the link, we have lost our strength. We can never do as much divided as we can do united with God. Each one of us is a part of the House of

Charity family. So let's never forget where we came from. Today, then, make the decision, by our discussion, our fellowship and this seminar to be a good member of the House of Charity family, the House of Charity team."

Chapter 47

Brother begs so that others may eat

Headline of a six column story from the April 20, 1979 Minneapolis Star on the occasion of the 50th birthday of the founder.

Brother celebrated his 50th birthday by taking 10,000 pounds of noodles, rice and candy to the poverty-stricken people of Haiti. The happiness in the faces of the little black children, as he gave them food, always lifted his spirits. His overseas apostolate was now called the Mission of Mercy.

When Brother de Paul had reached 40, he had had a difficult time accepting the fact that he was no longer "young." Through his 40's, an old family friend, Catherine Erpelding, said laughingly, "Brother has changed. He's decided he wanted to 'loosen up.' It took him 20 years to get this sense of humor!" Toward the end of his 40's he abandoned his rigid butch haircut and had his silver hair styled.

Now that he was 50, he had come to grips with his mid-life transition. He could accept a slower pace and he even asked the board of directors to help find an administrator to help him coordinate the work of the House of Charity. As a tribute to Brother de Paul on his 50th birthday, WCCO-TV presented his movie "25¢ and God."

For 27 years he had lived 24 hours a day, seven days a week on the premises, sharing the work, the meals, the problems and disturbances at night. Years ago, Dr. Spano had urged Brother to find separate living quarters, but he had felt the House of Charity was his home. Now his doctors insisted. On August 1, 1979 he moved to a studio apartment and according to Brother, "It was a painful and traumatic move, but it will be good for me physically and emotionally." He had learned to say goodbye to buildings before but not to the love and security of his House of Charity family.

Grace Fanning, the 84-year old volunteer who insisted on scrubbing the floors on her knees, moved into Brother's former quarters at the House of Charity. As of this writing, she's still scrubbing floors!

About the time of his move, Brother got a notice that the House of Bargains was being evicted after 10 years on West Broadway. The Troubadors had lost one of their stores in a fire and now they faced eviction. They decided to sell everything in the store and start their "Special Shoppe" with newly donated second-hand merchandise in the basement of the House of Charity on Eighth Street. It would be a much smaller store, but once again, after 10 years, they would be back at the House of Charity. After spending over $8,000 in the store's account for remodeling and furnishings, Brother de Paul and the Troubadors had a special service, and a blessing of the new store on Wednesday and a Grand Opening on Friday, October 19, 1979. They were back in business raising money for the House of Charity.

For the last five years, Brother de Paul had been suffering from a painful neurological condition that started in his thighs and spread to his feet. He also had problems with his bladder that prevented a full night's sleep. He visited the Mayo Clinic, but the pains continued. He felt exhausted, "burned out" physically and emotionally. Once again, he begged the Board of Directors to help find someone who could help with the administration of the House of Charity.

He announced to them that beginning February 1, 1980, he would take a sabbatical leave for up to six months. "For my own emotional and physical health, I must not assume responsibility until I become more rested and relaxed and can then, by avoiding stress, eliminate some of the daily medications I have been taking for years. . . .

"Before I return I would like to assume a different role, a limited one — most likely raising funds, designing, remodeling, etc. as per my expertise of 28 years. I do no longer desire to be top administrator, though I would like to feel that I had input into policy and procedure of serving the poor."

In the spring of 1979 and 1980 the founder had major surgery. Always wanting to accomplish much, he found recuperation difficult.

Brother received one of the most touching offers of genuine Christian love at this trying time from Rev. Gordon Peterson, the pastor of Soul's Harbor in the former Nicollet Hotel. He called and offered Brother de Paul a free room for six months or as long as he needed it.

Brother remembered meeting him on the shores of Galilee many years ago when they were both in the Holy Land, and Rev. Peterson rushed over and gave him a big bear hug. Now he was putting his love and concern into deeds.

While Brother was away, trying to restore his physical, emotional and spiritual health, his staff carried on at the House of Charity. Alice Codden managed the office and was the "senior advisor," Fred Niederloh, the bookkeeper, continued to unscramble the debits and credits. Ethel Fredrickson, worked in the mail room getting the letters out and keeping the mailing list up to date. Gary Bonin took care of the telephones after office hours besides being a chauffeur and general office helper, Tom Pederson was the resident coordinator, Don Lebak did his usual good job of supervising the Food Centre and Bob, the cook, worked with his crew to produce the meals six days a week. This staff met once a week to plan ahead, to iron out any difficulties and to "carry on with his work for the poor as Brother would want us to." Don Le Roy handled the separate housing department.

On May 1, 1980, the Board of Directors acquired an administrator to supervise the work of the House of Charity. He had a degree in Social Service with specialized studies in economics, accounting, human services plus hotel administration. He had worked in the hotel business and had felt a commitment to help and serve people. For years the founder had requested a helper to enable him to work more with people and less administration, but the board had their own ideas. Yet it was always the difference in philosophy which caused the internal problems.

When Brother de Paul, because the operating funds were dangerously low, returned to work at the end of May, his job was reduced to fund raising and the public relations activities he had managed before. He continued his practice, started in 1954, of sending birthday cards to over 600 shut-ins all over the world. Among the letters he received from these people was one from Patricia: "Once again your thoughtful greeting raised my spirits on a very special day. It was not only my birthday but my 30th wedding anniversary. . . .

"The disease that crippled me 25 years ago has helped me and my family to keep secular things in perspective. We have never had much money but there has always been a lot of love and we were able to realize that that was the important thing.

"Thank you for being a part of that expression of love through the years. It meant a lot. There were several times when your card was the only one I got. It was important to me that someone cared."

Even though the Board of Directors wanted to put the House of Charity on a firm business foundation, Brother de Paul wrote to the staff:

"For over 28 years we have tried to practice trust in Divine Providence to care and provide for *all* of our needs here at the House of Charity . . . this belief and philosophy has become the strong foundation of our apostolate. Despite some 'pinches' God has never failed us, but He expects us to use the wisdom and experience of these 28 years, combined with this beautiful trust."

His summer appeal letter brought in enough to keep them afloat until the big Christmas drive.

With his fund-raising taken care of, Brother de Paul turned to his other love and took a group of seven people to Haiti to show them where and how his Mission of Mercy worked. They didn't go empty handed. With help from many friends in the Twin Cities, the group brought vitamins, aspirin, seeds and noodles plus candy and whistles for the children.

Haiti is the poorest country in the Western Hemisphere with nearly six million people squeezed into land the size of Maryland. Eighty percent of the Haitians live in the countryside in conditions little changed from their great-grandparents. They suffer poverty, hunger, disease and illiteracy. Their average income for a year is $125.

Just before Brother de Paul's group arrived, Haiti had been hit by Hurricane Allen which devastated many of their shacks and ruined the little food they were growing. When Brother saw this, he sent 20,000 pounds of food to them in a chartered plane.

Father John McMillan, an Episcopalian priest from St. Nicholas Church in Richfield, Minnesota, travelled with the group and when he was asked his thoughts about Haiti, said, "These are memories that will never leave. We must hope and pray that somehow we can do more than just put bandaids on the gaping wounds in this country." His church built a school there.

These Mission of Mercy trips were tiring and heart-rending for Brother, but each time he brought a group to Haiti, he felt he had introduced the plight of the Haitians to people who could help them.

Don Lebak, in charge of the Food Centre for years, chats with our friend, Rev. J. Millard Ahlstrom, in chapel before Don's retirement worship service.

BROTHER DE PAUL LOVES CHILDREN EVERYWHERE . . .
and THEY LOVE HIM.

Minneapolis children surround him — with candy baskets he gave them for Easter in 1953.

Founder hugs a baby at Minneapolis FOOD CENTRE.

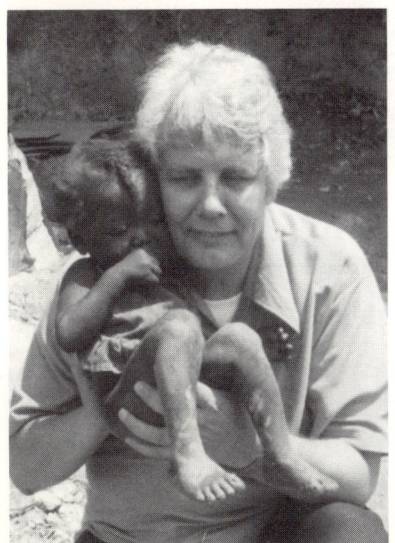
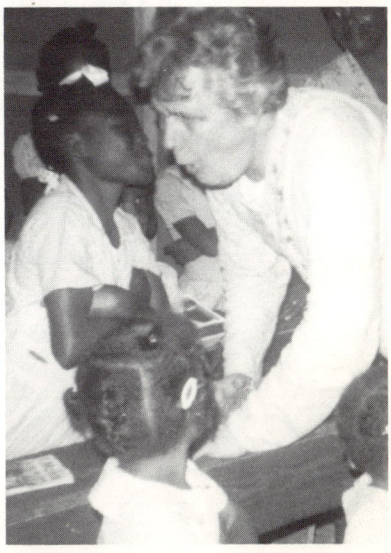

He holds a beautiful little girl in Haiti, near death, suffering from malnutrition.

In one of the schools in Haiti where he feeds the students, a young girl gives him a kiss, in appreciation.

Youngsters anywhere in the world always bring a beaming smile to the founder.

Chapter 48

Every September Brother de Paul gathered the staff, the volunteers, the residents and friends to celebrate Alice Codden's birthday. She had been his secretary, his friend, his right arm for over 25 years and now he wanted to especially honor her on her 80th birthday. She had given so much of herself to the House of Charity — working overtime most of the time, overseeing the Christmas Cheer Project, giving up her salary, but not her work, when she went on Social Security, sharing the good times and the bad.

An overflow crowd enthusiastically applauded Alice as she entered the chapel — they had come to share their prayers, their love and their appreciation. The "Big Kids," a Lutheran group that had sung at the House of Charity for many years, sang "Hallelujah Day." Episcopal Father Richard K. Smith, a long-time friend, gave the homily, using Alice's name to tell of her qualities. A - able, l - loving, i - industrious, c - careful, e - empathetic. She was all these when she came 25 years ago and she had these same qualities now. When she thanked her friends for coming, she told them, "The way I feel tonight, I think 81 will be a cinch! Retirement is definitely not for me."

As Henry Johnson, one of the volunteers wrote, "Welcome, Alice, to the Octogenarian Club."

Two weeks after celebrating Alice's 80th birthday, Brother de Paul gave a loving tribute at the Wednesday Ecumenical Service to Rev. Dr. and Mrs. Forrest Richeson. "In deep appreciation for his 50 years in the ministry of the Lord and in genuine gratitude for their friendship and their encouragement of our work at the House of Charity and our overseas work."

Rev. Richeson had been pastor of the First Christian Church of Minneapolis and had also given 35 years of spiritual direction to Alcoholics Anonymous. He listened to thousands of Fifth step inventories from alcoholics all over the state.

To surprise the Richesons at this prayer service, Brother had invited his successor at First Christian Church, Rev. Tom Shifflet, to give the homily. His former assistant, Rev. L. G. Parkhurst, came from Rochester, Minnesota to read from Scripture and share in the prayers. After the service they all went out for dinner and more fellowship. It was an evening of warmth and love. Denominational barriers came down one by one.

Brother de Paul liked his role in service better than he liked administration. He was a "people person" and he enjoyed planning and giving these evenings of tribute to those he loved. Birthday parties were given for many "little people," too.

On November 29, 1980, Dorothy Day died. She had been Brother de Paul's friend and inspiration for over 25 years. She believed that to fail to love the most despised of human beings is to fail to love Jesus. Her co-worker, Peter Maurin, had said, "What we give to the poor for Christ's sake is what we carry with us when we die."

Materially, Dorothy Day had nothing. She lived next door to a shopping-bag lady in a settlement house in Manhattan's Lower East Side. She was buried in the cast-off clothing she had always worn. Her casket was a simple pine box which she had used as a storage chest for the last 40 years. Her funeral service was very simple as she would have wanted. In her death, she would carry much with her for all she gave to Christ's poor.

Brother de Paul was in Haiti with his Mission of Mercy, so he had no word of Dorothy Day's death until he returned to Minneapolis. He had lost a saintly co-worker for the poor.

Chapter
49

On January 20, 1981, Ronald Reagan was sworn in as the 40th President of the United States, and the whole world rejoiced at the release of the American hostages in Iran. That same day, yellow ribbons were tied around everything possible to let the hostages know they were loved. Brother de Paul used his big sign on the front of the House of Charity, "Welcome home 52 Americans with our love and prayers." A yellow ribbon surrounded the sign. The Tribune carried the photo of the lighted sign on the front page.

With the new administrator some changes took place. Brother de Paul did not object to every change, but he felt they were running the House of Charity as a business rather than an organization helping with God's work. Brother knew that changes were always necessary as he had himself instituted many over the 30 years, but certain basic philosophies must remain unchanged. The founder would never approve of the House of Charity being swallowed up by another organization nor becoming a part of any one denomination. So the tensions increased steadily.

Brother knew he had been operating for all of these years by depending on the providence of God. He didn't think dedication could be purchased; his staff had worked endless hours for small salaries because they believed in his work. He was totally aware of the high cost of living, but he knew that salaries did not make better workers.

Some wanted to buy some food items to make the meals at the Food Centre more balanced. Brother de Paul had always prided himself in the fact that "all food is donated. We make no purchases of any kind for the meals; promote more to get better and more food."

Because the founder was deeply grateful for every gift, he sent a thank you card or letter to every benefactor as soon as possible.

The Housing Department or Hotel was a separate function of the House of Charity — as far as Brother de Paul was concerned. He felt that the Housing Department should reimburse the House of Charity for any use of its equipment, services, or staff. He would assume responsibility for raising funds for only the non-profit aspect of the apostolate.

The board meetings were substantially matters of finance, payroll, bills, grants, etc. Although there were other items on the agenda, discussion about the poor was short. It appeared to the founder as if it were the meeting of a big business corporation.

Twice in the summer of 1981 Brother de Paul was in the hospital for tests to determine whether he needed abdominal surgery. He had contracted a virus infection while in Haiti and this led to constant chills, headaches, fever, stomach cramps and diarrhea. A diagnosis was difficult, even at Mayo Clinic, but by treating the symptoms, the "unknown tropical disease" lessened its grip.

Whenever Brother faced physical or emotional setbacks, it seemed something happened to raise his spirits. This time it was his 52nd birthday celebration. At the Wednesday evening Scripture Service, his youngest sister, Vonnie, invited his family, his friends, his radio audience to join in a prayer of thanksgiving for all God's blessings on her brother.

Father Richard K. Smith, one of Brother's Episcopalian friends, was the Master of Ceremonies. He recalled the year 1929, "the stock market crash and the birth of Tom Kondrak. One was a disaster; the other one of the great things that happened for us here in this community."

Father John McMillan, the Episcopalian priest who went to Haiti with Brother last November, led the prayer. "On this occasion, Lord, we want to ask you to bless him and to help him so to number his days so that he will have many, many more years in which to serve you. Would you let him know today and all the days of his life that you walk the ways of this world beside him, being always there to lift him up should he stumble and to encourage him while he stands. We offer these prayers in the name of the risen Christ. Amen."

The Reverend Glen Hendrix, pastor of the First Free Methodist Church, and Father Stan Maslowski of Our Lady of Perpetual Help Church both spoke of Brother de Paul's long struggle to take care of Christ's poor.

Anatoli prayed the Lord's Prayer in the old Russian language. When Brother de Paul providentially had been in Rome in February, 1979, he had met Anatoli, a religious refugee, and had shown him a picture of the Catholic priest he had visited in Leningrad 10 years earlier. It was Anatoli's pastor! He told Brother de Paul he was on his way to Minneapolis, Minnesota with his wife and son and daughter. They have been close friends ever since.

After Alice asked the congregation for prayers of petition and thanksgiving, she introduced Brother as the "Noodle Man," a name he acquired after shipping tons of noodles to Haiti.

Brother de Paul thanked everyone, but especially Don Lebak, who was retiring, for his many years of fantastic management of the Food Centre, and Rick Erickson for producing his radio shows. He reiterated his trust in God to continue providing food, funds and facilities for the House of Charity just as He had since the beginning with 25¢. Brother told his family and friends that "part of my heart is in Haiti."

After the birthday service, the North Suburban Auxiliary, with his sisters, Vonnie and Lucille as hostesses, served refreshments in the Alice Codden Lobby. Being with all these beautiful people he loved, Brother de Paul didn't mind turning 52.

A week later, the 1,000,000th caller dialed 529-9236 to hear Brother de Paul's Daily Inspirational Message. For seven and a half years, each day he used the media of today to bring a message that the caller could tie into daily living. On the Wednesday of the Ecumenical Scripture Service to commemorate the millionth call, Brother quoted Winston Churchill: "Never give up. Never give up. Never give up."

Many people let Brother know how much they appreciated his daily message. A Lutheran friend wrote: "God bless you for your daily words of inspiration. You have helped me in so many ways to face another day of pain. I will be going to the hospital for surgery on my eyes next month for the 24th time in 10 years."

Another listener wrote "How proud I am to share in the wealth of God's love you pour out on starving souls. Everyone is seeking God and inner peace."

Along with his daily recorded messages, Brother put a new thought on the House of Charity's outdoor sign each week: "Life is too short to be little." "Best sermons are with our lives, not our lips." "Greatest prayer is patience." "Better be faithful than famous." Each thought seemed to be a message to himself.

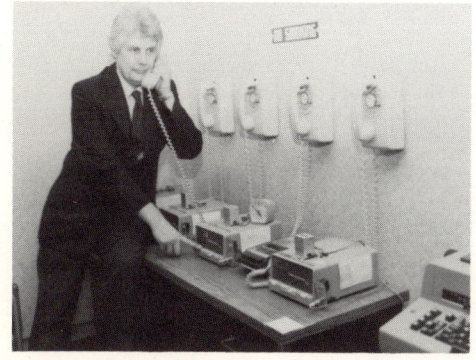

The founder answers the one millionth call to his daily inspirational phone messages.

OUTDOOR LIGHTED SIGN — and front of the building, looking downtown on a cold, wintry day.

Chapter 50

When the Minnesota State Legislature cut about 1900 people in Hennepin County from General Assistance benefits on July 1, 1981, the number of people needing free food and housing jumped considerably. The food shelves around the city were getting empty and the food lines at the Salvation Army's Harbor Light Center, the inner city churches like St. Stephen's, drop-in centers and the House of Charity Food Centre were getting longer. The number at the Food Centre was up surprisingly only about 1,000 a month. In July, the beginning of the 30th year for the House of Charity, Brother sent out his annual appeal for financial help, and in September he sent an S.O.S. to take care of the increased load.

Among his responses was a letter and a contribution from a former resident who had had a tough time giving up alcohol. He used to ask Brother "Why do you bother with guys like us? To do this work you must be nuts." Now he is happily married and doing this "nutty" work as a counselor in a detoxification center in Northern Minnesota. He wrote, "I haven't forgotten your love in my time of need so how could I forget you in yours?"

He also heard from former Brother Francis of Detroit. "Think of you and the House of Charity often. May not be able to help you much materially, but do with prayer. Would not trade the four years spent there for anything. The riches that I came away with are still bringing me rewards to this day. I learned much; was given much; and hope I am sharing much of that with others."

Besides begging for the House of Charity, Brother begged seeds for his Haitian friends. When several persons including Joe Hurston, a missionary in Haiti, received almost a ton of seeds from the Mission of Mercy, he wrote, "We can make wonderful use of them. I'm planning a big trip out to the remote regions in the near future and these seeds will be a tremendous blessing to our isolated brothers and sisters."

Although Brother de Paul had divested himself of the day to day management of the House of Charity and the Food Centre, he still raised most of the funds. He also tried to settle the long time grievances of the Troubadors, the volunteers who had run the House of Bargains for 25 years. They had written to the Board of Directors a year ago, asking to be represented and they had had no reply. Now that they were back on the premises, they felt they were losing their independence. They wanted to pay rent for the store, their Special Shoppe, run it their own way, control and vote on their own finances and they wanted a reply, aye or nay, from the board. The board posted a letter on the wall in the Special Shoppe asking for the Troubadors' cooperation. The girls felt they had cooperated all these years and deserved a more specific answer.

In the fall of 1981, the founder made another trip to the Mayo Clinic for a checkup and besides getting his diagnosis, he had a chance to visit with Rev. Dr. Billy Graham. Mrs. Graham was having surgery. Brother de Paul had met this world famous evangelist years before at a downtown Minneapolis Kiwanis club anniversary, but now he spent a few minutes sharing again. "He was very nice, a great listener. He was very gracious. My short visit with him is one of the treasures of my life."

On Sunday, October 25, 1981, Brother de Paul gathered about 300 friends to celebrate the 30th anniversary of his founding of the House of Charity. Besides inviting the volunteers, the residents, the benefactors, the clergy and his family, he chose this occasion to pay "a loving tribute to the handicapped." Rev. David Meisner, a Lutheran minister, delivered a stirring message from his wheelchair. Betty Zaczek, who had shared her singing talent for many years, sang "My God and I" from her wheelchair where she's been confined for 36 years. She was joined by Peggy LaBerge who has been blind since birth, and Dick Akehurst, playing the organ.

Amid the corsages, balloons, food and dancers — threading their way among the wheelchairs with the blind leading the blind through the dance steps, everyone felt the warmth and love that had been built up through the 30 years. Brother de Paul was in his glory when he could get people together like this.

On Thanksgiving Eve he continued the 30th anniversary celebration with an ecumenical service "to thank God together for each other." For many years Christmas cans were put in restaurants and stores to collect money to help pay for the House of Charity Christmas projects. Once again Steve and Janet Rasmussen and Patty Emilson distributed the cans to helpers at the Thanksgiving Eve services.

The Rev. Dr. William Berg, one of Brother's many Lutheran friends, was the homilist. He was grateful this Thanksgiving for Brother de Paul, "someone who not only talks about needs but does something about them.

"Somebody said 'I was hungry' and you formed a humanity club to discuss my hunger. Jesus said 'I was hungry and you gave me food.'

"Someone said, 'I was in prison and you went to your prayer meeting to pray for my release.' Jesus said 'I was in prison and you visited me.'

"Someone said 'I was sick and you went off and thanked God for your good health.' Jesus said 'I was sick and you ministered unto me.'

"Someone said 'I was naked and you debated the morality of my appearance.' Jesus said 'I was naked and you clothed me.' 'I was homeless and you took me in.'

"This is the power of this ministry, Jesus Christ, who gave everything for us."

Because of inflation, unemployment and the new legislation against General assistance, there were more and more people who were hungry and homeless. Now that winter was here their plight was even more desperate. As many as nine small shelters were opened in various churches and neighborhood houses and the Board of Directors of the House of Charity asked the United Way for $178,210 to support sleeping quarters for 53 people each night for one year. After giving free housing for 30 years, it was an entirely new concept to be paid for housing the needy.

Brother de Paul had fought the idea of accepting money from the United Way or any institutionalized church from the beginning, and he was against it now. "We've always paid for the homeless to stay at the St. Andrew's Hotel or the 'Y.' We never turned anyone down in all these years. We're not in the hotel business. They even gave eviction notices to people who had lived in the building for years—even before it became the House of Charity."

One of the officers of the Good Samaritan League at their Christmas party asked, "Why should we raise money when grants bring in such big amounts?" Many others would ask the same question.

But Brother de Paul still went to Haiti for his 4th annual Christmas party for missionaries. He had met and worked with missionaries from many churches, but many of these people did not know each other until he invited them to his Christmas parties. During the roll call, 10 countries were represented, 17 states and 16 religions — all bound together by their belief in Jesus Christ and their service to the poor. Reverend Phil Hansen, a Lutheran who had spoken many times in the Minneapolis chapel and who works with chemically dependent people, was the speaker and he commented, "Only Brother de Paul could bring all of these people together . . . history is being made at this party."

Reverend Hoover T. Grimsby, senior pastor of the downtown Central Lutheran Church, a neighbor, wrote in a letter to the editors column of the Minneapolis Tribune about the founder of the House of Charity, "It is hard to believe that one person can be as effective and influential as he has been over so many years . . . we have so much darkness around us that it is good to have a person lighting candles to expel the darkness."

The House of Charity Christmas traditions were kept intact. Alice supervised the packaging of each gift for thousands of prisoners, and for the mentally and physically ill. The thank you notes included one from an 18-year old who was serving time in the St. Cloud Reformatory. He had been an orphan since age four and had spent most of his life in foster and group homes. "I worry about my future when I leave here. I don't want to get into any more trouble. I want to live a happy life and be a good person. . . . It helps if you have someone to care about you."

On Christmas Eve, Christmas night and New Year's Eve the ecumenical chapel was the setting for mass, for caroling, for the candlelight service, for fellowship and refreshments. This cozy, carpeted chapel with the beamed ceiling, the stained glass windows, the beautiful wood pulpit and altar, the wooden crucifix from Oberammergau, the white flocked tree with red balls, the red candelabra, the poinsettias all were a fitting background for the almost life-size figures of Jesus, Mary, and Joseph.

As Brother de Paul spent his hour of prayer alone in this beautiful Christmas setting, he remembered his Christmas 30 years ago when he and Brother Martin shared their little dining room with 75 hungry men, feeding them six of them at a time. Seventeen men then had wrapped themselves in their overcoats and had slept on the cold floor. When his thoughts returned to the present, he prayed, "My God, what you have done with that first twenty-five cents!!! WHERE DO WE GO FROM HERE?"

In the Minneapolis Tribune on November 14, 1981, Robert S. Lyle wrote on the editorial page:

> "If you run short of role models for bootstrap jobs, consider Brother de Paul, the tireless charity worker . . . this man has performed miracles in the last 30 years, by providing food and clothing for thousands of indigent street people . . . has operated without help from church or government. . . . But the corsages, balloons and dancing cheered him (at his anniversary party for the handicapped). . . . It was as if the bread he has cast on the water all these years was at last coming back to him."

HOT AND VERY THIRSTY . . . very unsafe to drink the local water . . . founder's first attempt to handle a coconut in the jungle.

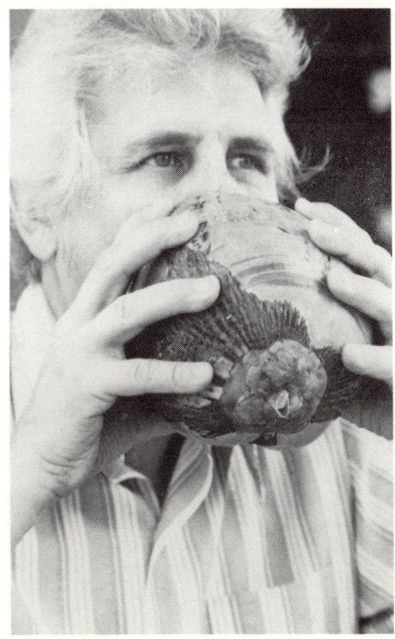

The Founders' Postlude . . .

30,000 feet above the Atlantic Ocean in a super jet . . . rainbow of thots . . . July, 1982. . . . I have just taken the manuscript of this book to dedicate it at the shrine of Fatima in Portugal . . . had twelve wonderful days and nights of intense, powerful prayer and renewal. . . . How can I ever forget my first trans Atlantic crossing . . . when I was in college in 1949 . . . my travellers cheques were either lost or stolen . . . at our refueling stop in the Azores . . . arriving frightened at night at my very first overseas stop, the Lisbon airport, with only $3.87 in my pocket . . . all alone in a strange foreign country . . . what training to trust in Divine Providence! . . . I thought of John whom I met just before I left Minneapolis, while I was sitting on a bench waiting for a city bus . . . his breath still stale from "booze" . . . he had been with us as a resident several times . . . an alcoholic and a prisoner . . . very talented . . . we had his wedding and reception at northside House of Charity on a humid day with temperature in the high nineties . . . our good benefactor, Rev. John Propert, our Baptist brother, officiating . . . that same group — of loyal members of "our family" who always wanted to help these events to be very special — participated. . . . How wonderful to have such beautiful supporters!! . . .

Then along came Ernie, who had lived with us many times . . . just out of a treatment center where he had been for a year . . . recall him being set afire by ignorant but cruel teenagers near the Mississippi River, because he was "one of those useless bums" . . . and then his long, painful recovery . . . both really great guys . . . both fabulous salesmen at the rummage sales which the residents sponsored for several years, on the honor system, raising thousands of dollars to keep their home in operation . . . yet they struggle daily to keep their "heads up high." . . .

I ponder, too, that "miraculously" during these 30 years not a hand has been lifted to me in violence . . . which brings to mind Arnie, a native American (Indian), who told me he would "kill anyone" who would try to hurt me . . . he and his wife ate at our Food Centre for years. . . . I think now of the millions of times we have fed Christ . . . realizing that it was Christ Himself who said that if we feed "the least," that we actually feed Him. . . .

The time of prayer at Fatima re-imprinted on me and re-impressed me, that my life's calling is to feed the hungry . . . where ever the hungry may be . . . without any human boundaries. . . . I have to be hungry only a little while, to realize how tragic and painful and degrading are the gnawing pangs of an empty stomach.

And how about the millions of dollars, the food, the clothing, the medicines, the services, etc. that GOD, in His Providence, used little me to solicit for the needy. . . .

I come back relaxed and refreshed and revitalized . . . am on my way home?? But where is my home? Minneapolis . . . Fatima . . . Haiti . . . Korea . . . (in jails, workhouses, prisons, nursing homes, hospitals) . . . ? ? ? . . . where ever God directs to my brothers and sisters who are hurting and in need . . . in body, mind, soul . . . how many times I have crossed the seas or opened the bars of a prison cell to live my mission. . . .

Often I wonder where the young Arab is . . . met him in the prison in Copenhagen, Denmark in 1971 . . . he had converted to Christianity and took the name Alphonso . . . what surprised me was that he had worked several years before that at the distinguished Charlie's Cafe Exceptionale (now closed) in downtown Minneapolis.

On the day of my return to Minneapolis . . . lying on a stretcher in the emergency room of North Memorial Hospital . . . waiting for the x-ray reports. . . . I had accidentally slipped, banging my left hip consecutively on four stairs. . . . A broken hip? . . . a cast? A long time of recuperation and inactivity? . . . Amidst the pain . . . a prayer from the heart . . . God, you have taken care of me throughout my life . . . Help me again to trust you as a loving, caring, concerned Divine "Daddy" . . . . . . one more time.

CHAPEL AT CHRISTMAS TIME. Alice Codden, office manager and the founder's secretary, contemplates the nativity scene, always the center of holiday worship and activities for the poor.

ON THE STREETS OF JERUSALEM. Pilgrimages to the Holy Land include the unique practice of carrying a wooden cross, an experience never forgotten by those people travelling with Brother de Paul.

HUGGING IN THE CHAPEL. The founder's nephew and niece, Scott and Leslie Strandberg, cling to him before one of his overseas jaunts.

One of the well wishers embraces him during the closing hymn, "How Great Thou Art."

The sisters of the founder, Vonnie Strandberg and Lucille Kondrak, pose in a rare photograph together at one of his birthday celebrations.

HANDICAPPED AND SENIORS

Both are special loves of Brother de Paul. At the annual HANDICAPPED PARTY he enjoys chatting with Ethel Casteel. A thrilled 87 year "young" George Schneider told everyone, "This is the best birthday I ever had," after a birthday party was held in his honor.

Photos by Tom Pederson

TASTING THE HOT, NOURISHING FOOD. In the pioneer days the founder cooked for the hungry and in later years he checked the quality and flavor daily. Many times this food was his own meal, too.